DATE DUE		
BC382		
Mar 27		
July 10		
July 24		
Feb. 19		

Prepared by the National Historic Parks and Sites Branch and published
under the authority
of the Hon. John Fraser, PC, MP,
Minister responsible for Parks Canada
Ottawa 1980
Editor: Bessie E. Silversides
Design Management: Eric Plummer
Design: Eiko Emori

Canadian Historic Sites: Occasional Papers in Archaeology and History
will be published as papers become available. Manuscripts may be
submitted to Chief, Research Division, National Historic Parks and Sites
Branch, Parks Canada, Environment Canada, Ottawa, Ontario K1A 1G2

Articles appearing in this series are abstracted and indexed in *Historica
Abstracts* and/or *America: History and Life*.

Second Empire Style in Canadian Architecture
by Christina Cameron and Janet Wright

Canadian Historic Sites:
Occasional Papers in Archaeology and History.
No. 24

Cover: Examples of Second Empire Style across Canada. Front: 201 Charles Street, Belleville, Ont. (*Photo by Gary Robertson, Technical Data Services Division, Engineering and Architecture Branch, Department of Indian and Northern Affairs*). Back: top left, 25 Winter Avenue, St. John's, Nfld (*Photo by John Bell, Technical Data Services Division, Engineering and Architecture Branch, Department of Indian and Northern Affairs*); top right, 507 Head Street, Esquimalt, B.C. (*Photo by Marcel Durand, Canadian Inventory of Historic Building, Parks Canada, Department of the Environment*); bottom left, former Post Office and Customs House, Fredericton, N.B. (*Canadian Inventory of Historic Building, Parks Canada, Department of the Environment*); bottom right, Victoria Block, Clinton, Ont. (*Photo by Gary Robertson, Technical Data Services Division, Engineering and Architecture Branch, Department of Indian and Northern Affairs*).

En français ce numéro s'intitule *Lieux historiques canadiens: cahiers
d'archéologie et d'histoire*, nº 24 (nº de catalogue R61-2/1-24F). En vente
au Canada par l'entremise de nos agents libraires agréés et autres
librairies, ou par la poste au: Centre d'édition du gouvernement du
Canada, Approvisionnements et Services Canada, Hull, Québec, Canada K1A 1G2.

Catalogue No.: R61-2/1-24
ISBN: 0-660-10446-6
Library of Congress Catalogue Card No.: 70-103875
QS-7098-000-EE-A1

Price Canada: **$10.00**
Price other countries: **$12.00**
Price subject to change without notice.

Second Empire Style in Canadian Architecture

by Christina Cameron and Janet Wright

Canadian Historic Sites
No. 24

6 Abstract
6 Preface
7 Acknowledgements
7 Introduction
8 Montreal City Hall: A Classic Canadian Example
9 Second Empire and Napoleon III of France
10 England: Early Advocate of Second Empire
11 Second Empire and the United States
12 Canada: Stirrings of Second Empire
13 Department of Public Works
15 Other Public Buildings
16 Commercial Building
17 Second Empire for Canadian Houses
18 Ontario Houses
19 Houses in the Atlantic Provinces
20 Quebec Houses
21 Houses in the Prairies
21 Houses in British Columbia
22 Conclusions
230 Appendix. List of Illustrations
232 Endnotes
238 Bibliography

Abstract

Second Empire as an architectural style is most easily recognized by its mansard or broken roof and its rich sculptural ornamentation. Originally associated with the court of Emperor Napoleon III of France, this florid style reached Canada by way of the United States and, to a lesser extent, via England. The most sophisticated examples of Second Empire design are to be found in major public and institutional buildings erected in Canada during the 1870s and 1880s. During this period, it became the height of fashion for domestic building, ranging in variety from high-style residences in the cities to simple vernacular interpretations in more remote areas of the country. By the end of the century, however, Second Empire, as an architectural style, ceased to influence Canadian architects and builders.

Submitted for publication 1977, by Christina Cameron and Janet Wrignt, Canadian Inventory of Historic Building, Parks Canada, Ottawa.

Preface

The Canadian Inventory of Historic Building is a computerized data system created to record Canada's architectural heritage. When the programme was established in 1970, its primary purpose was to provide a sampling of building across Canada that would serve as a comparative basis for assessment by the Historic Sites and Monuments Board of Canada. Phase 1 identified and recorded the exterior details of buildings from selected par of Canada. A sampling (not to exceed 10 per cent) of Phase 1 structures was then chosen for Phase 2 examination which involved the recording of interior detail. Within the sample areas, a cut-off date was assigned: pre-1880 in Ontario, Quebec and Atlantic provinces; pre-1914 in northern and western Canada. This was necessary to accommodate the survey to available resources, but it was recognized that eventually the Canadian Inventory of Historic Building would have to update its record to include post-1880 buildings in the east. To date, Phase 1 has 180,000 recorded structures, and Phase 2 has 2,000 recorded buildings.

This present study is a pilot project which attempts to identify, analyse and interpret the architectural data stored in the Canadian Inventory of Historic Building computer. Following a preliminary research phase, during which secondary and accessible primary sources were consulted, the mansard roof was identifie as an essential part of the Second Empire style. The Canadian Inventory of Historic Building computer then produced printouts of all buildings recorded as having mansard roofs, separated by building use (residential and non-residential). The results of the visual screening of the photo cards identified in the compute search allowed the formulation of certain hypotheses about the Second Empire style in Canada. These ideas were tested again archival photographs of demolished buildings (for these are obviously not recorded by the Canadian Inventory of Historic Building if they disappeared before 1970), and documentary research to produce the present study. It is hoped that the finding will make a useful contribution to our understanding and apprec ation of Canada's architectural heritage.

A collection of slides of Second Empire buildings in Canada is being prepared in conjunction with the National Film Board.

Acknowledgements

To produce a study of this kind, the authors had to consult personnel of many public archives and research institutions, all of whom have given their full cooperation. The authors are most indebted to the late Mathilde Brosseau, for her participation in the initial phase of this project and her help in establishing its overall direction. The authors also wish to express their thanks to the many persons who added pieces to the puzzle with patience and enthusiasm: Ella Chase, Emerson, Manitoba; Gordon Couling, Guelph, Ontario; Sister Gabriel Cummins, Calgary, Alberta; Marie-Jeanne Daigneau, Sherbrooke, Quebec; James Dickhout, Lowbanks, Ontario; Lynne DiStefano, London, Ontario; Lionel Dorge, Saint Boniface, Manitoba; Donna Dul, Winnipeg, Manitoba; Marcel Durand, Montreal, Quebec; Simon Fortin, Saint-Jean-Port-Joli, Quebec; Lois Foster, Belleville, Ontario; Gerald Fremlin, Clinton, Ontario; Hastings County Historical Society, Belleville, Ontario; Martha Ann Kidd, Peterborough, Ontario; Georges Gauthier-Larouche, Quebec, Quebec; Mr. and Mrs. Gordon Glenn, Indian Head, Saskatchewan; Yves Laliberté, Quebec, Quebec; Robert Lemire, Montreal, Quebec; Martin Lewis, Belleville, Ontario; Anne Little, Toronto, Ontario; John Lutman, London, Ontario; G. Edward Mills, Vancouver, British Columbia; Iris Moffat, Cowansville, Quebec; Olive Newcombe and the Dundas Historical Society Museum, Dundas, Ontario; Niagara County Historical Museum, Niagara-on-the-Lake, Ontario; Shane O'Dea, Saint John's, Newfoundland; Jean Perchat, Sainte-Marie-de-Beauce, Quebec; Trevor Powell, Regina, Saskatchewan; Terry Reksten, Victoria, British Columbia; Douglas Richardson, Toronto, Ontario; Randy R. Rostecki, Winnipeg, Manitoba; Charles Stuart, Rivière-du-Loup, Quebec; C. James Taylor, Ottawa, Ontario; Ann Thomas, Ottawa, Ontario; Christopher Thomas, Toronto, Ontario; William Thompson, Winnipeg, Manitoba; Jean Westwell, Belleville, Ontario.

Introduction

It is difficult to determine precisely when the name "Second Empire" became attached to a particular architectural style. While architectural historians writing after World War II almost invariably use the term "Second Empire" or "International Second Empire" to refer to ornate mansard-roofed designs of the third quarter of the 19th century,[1] contemporary observers never once referred to it as "Second Empire."

Admittedly, these writers were often conscious that the roots of the style lay in the Second Empire of Napoleon III of France, but they chose a variety of terms to describe it. In Canadian literature of the 1870s, we find a broad range of labels. Journalists writing in the *Canadian Illustrated News* described such buildings as "Renaissance" or "Palladian" or, interestingly enough, "in the modern French style of architecture."[2] The chief architect of the Department of Public Works in his annual reports gives different stylistic names to buildings of similar Second Empire design including "Italian" (his favourite choice), "Renaissance," "Italian Renaissance," "classic," "modern classic," and "free classic."[3]

American writers were as conscious as their Canadian counterparts of the "Renaissance" or "Italian" aspect of the style, but they tended to be more aware of the French connection. American pattern books often illustrated designs for what they called "French-Roof Cottages," "Anglo-French Cottages," "Anglo-French Villas" and "French-Italian suburban residences."[4] Certain contemporary writers were even more articulate in their assessment of the style. In 1866 the committee responsible for the construction of Boston City Hall stated that the new public building "may be described as the Italian *Renaissance*, modified and elaborated by the taste of the French architects of the last thirty years."[5] Two years later, John Kennion, commenting on modern buildings in New York City, made a similar analysis, by stating that "the style ... is what should justly be called the *Franco Italian*, or in other words, a French adaptation of the Italian style."[6] But it is in his description of the new Albany state capitol that Kennion achieved the definitive contemporary statement.

It is designed in the Renaissance, or modern French style of architecture, a style which will at once be recognized by those conversant with the subject as the prevailing mode of modern Europe, and one which the taste of the present Emperor of France in particular aided by the numerous and able staff of government architects, has for some years so largely illustrated in most of the renowned modern works of the French capital. Derived originally from Italian sources, and partially from the late edifices of the Venetian republic, this beautiful style has now been so successfully naturalized in other countries as to have become, in fact, the prevailing manner for most of those secular edifices of a dignified and permanent character which the wants of our times have called forth.[7]

To select a single 19th century term to describe this style would be a difficult task. From the wealth of labels proposed by contemporary writers, two prevailing themes emerge: the Renaissance aspect and the French aspect. While recognizing that the term "Second Empire" is indeed a modern one, we have chosen it as the most comprehensive and universally accepted term to describe this particular stylistic manifestation.

The Second Empire style is most readily identified by the mansard or broken roof (the "French" ingredient noted by contemporary writers) combined with a rich classicizing treatment of the façade, often with superimposed columns and sculptural decoration (the "Renaissance" factor). The earliest versions of this florid style began to appear in major Canadian cities in the late 1860s. During the 1870s, these ornate buildings took Canada by storm; but by the mid-1880s, after a rapid fall from fashion, they were no longer being erected.

During the period that Second Empire triumphed, it was considered to be particularly appropriate for institutions and public buildings (just as Gothic Revival at the same time was the only correct style for religious structures). By association, Second Empire became one of the acceptable styles for urban residences of the bourgeoisie. Although the style itself did not really change during its two-decade domination, the scale and degree of ornamentation varied enormously, depending on such factors as function, client, availability of materials, craftsmen, and established local traditions of building.

The Canadian Inventory of Historic Building, with its data bank of over 180,000 recorded buildings, has proved to be a useful tool in tracing the influence of the style across Canada. In its formal dress, the Second Empire style crossed local, provincial and even national boundaries, and in this sense was truly "international." But when this official form encountered regional customs and conditions, the resulting designs offer a variety of charming and individual solutions. The Canadian Inventory of Historic Building has made it possible to identify this more informal and distinctly Canadian aspect of the Second Empire style.

Montreal City Hall: A Classic Canadian Example

Before examining the historic roots of the Second Empire style, let us look in detail at a formal Canadian example, Montreal City Hall (Fig. 1). As it was originally conceived in 1872 by architect H.M. Perrault, this public building illustrates the basic elements of Second Empire design; namely, mansard roof, pavilion massing, classicizing ornamentation and consciousness of urban setting.

The mansard roof, a double-sloped or broken roof with steep lower slope and flatter shorter upper portion, was introduced in France in the 17th century. Named after François Mansart (1598–1666), the architect who introduced it in France, the mansard roof has a complex construction method. Unlike the framework for gable roofs which calls for single unbroken rafters, mansard roofs require two rafters for the different slopes. To increase the complexity still more, the pitch of each slope necessitates a different kind of material to cover it.

The appearance of the French or mansard roof in Canada[1] coincided with a significant factor in mid-19th century taste, namely the increased desire for picturesque effect. In the case of Montreal City Hall, the mansard roof and mansarded towers create a lively uneven silhouette. The picturesque effect thus achieved is enhanced by flagpoles, ornate dormer windows and decorative iron cresting along the tops of the various roofs.

In the arrangement of the building's mass into distinct units called "pavilions," Montreal City Hall adopts another common Second Empire device. Architects used this pavilion system in part to relieve the monotony of long uninterrupted wall surfaces and in part to indicate on the exterior the major internal divisions and functions of the building. In the case of Montreal City Hall, the articulation of the façade into distinct sections is the outward translation of the interior arrangement, as exemplified by the pronounced central pavilion, which indicates the main entrance and hall. The projecting and recessing planes of the wall surface accentuated by ornate mansarded towers, contribute to the picturesque quality of the design.

In addition to the mansard roof and pavilion massing, the classicizing ornamentation of the wall surface illustrates another characteristic feature of the Second Empire style. Although the decorative details have been borrowed indiscriminately from earlier architectural periods, the most important sources remain the classical styles as filtered through Italy. The use of superimposed columns and pilasters, often combined with pronounced string courses to create a grid-like pattern, may be said to stem from Italian Renaissance prototypes. On the other hand, the rich sculptural treatment of features like the monumental entrance to Montreal City Hall approaches the robust decoration of the Italian Baroque tradition. This dependence on Italian classical sources explains contemporary references to the style as "Renaissance" or "Italian."

Buildings designed in the Second Empire style often show a distinct consciousness of setting. Montreal City Hall is no exception, perched as it is on a height of land overlooking Place Jacques Cartier in front and the Champs de Mars behind. Simultaneously, it acts as a companion piece for the Court House across the small square to one side. Each outer wall offers a grandiose façade as an appropriate completion for the urban space. In addition to exploiting the potential of the site, Montreal City Hall also afforded exceptional panoramic views from within the building. One 19th century observer, remarking on its attractive setting, wrote that one could "see the main wharfs of the river navigation companies, Saint Helen's Island and the other side of the Saint Lawrence River."[2]

The City Hall was greeted with lavish praise in *L'Opinion publique*, January 24, 1878: "Construit à côté du Palais de Justice, sur la colline qui domine la place Jacques-Cartier, ce monument offre le plus riant coup-d'oeil et ne déparerait pas les plus belles villes du continent." A note of criticism, however, was added to this description: "Il est seulement regrettable qu'il ait pour vis-à-vis les plus détestables masures qui se puissent voir. Espérons que le gouvernement provincial, à qui appartiennent ces vielles baraques, les remplacera bientôt par de magnifiques bâtisses ...." The "old hovels" which are so disdainfully referred to would have included the Château de Ramezay, one of the finest and few remaining examples of urban building in Montreal from the French régime. Fortunately this advice was never followed but it does serve to characterize the "progressive" spirit of the age which advocated throwing out the old and building something that was newer and bigger and therefore better.

Second Empire and Napoleon III of France

Second Empire style takes its name from the Second Empire of Napoleon III of France. During his reign, which began in 1852 and terminated abruptly in 1870, the emperor and his wife, the Empress Eugénie, sought to make their court the cosmopolitan centre of fashion. It is not a mere accident that two of the first four international exhibitions took place in Paris during the Second Empire, in 1855 and 1867,[1] the earlier one being honoured by the presence of Queen Victoria and the Prince Consort of England.[2]

Determined to establish his capital as the symbol of his power, Napoleon III found himself a brilliant accomplice in the person of Baron Georges Haussmann whom he named Prefect of the Seine: together they undertook a vast programme of public works that in less than 20 years transformed the face of Paris. In addition to strictly functional projects such as the improvement of the sewer system and the distribution of drinking water, they carried out broad schemes of urban planning. Several slum districts were razed to make way for the famous network of boulevards and wide avenues:[3] parks and squares were created to offer oases of greenery in the heart of the city.

This programme did not escape notice. Enthusiastically endorsing Napoleon III's efforts, a contemporary American observer reported,

the present Emperor spends enormous sums in beautifying his capital and provincial cities; old quarters have been demolished, new boulevards have been cut through, streets widened and extended, elegant and costly residences replace those torn down, the Louvre extended and connected with the Tuileries, a Grand Hotel, a new Grand Opera House, churches, and public offices; all upon a scale of magnificence heretofore unknown, astonish the visitor at every turn.[4]

In this urban renewal programme, the most significant building – the building that would become for the outside world the symbol of Napoleon III's Paris – was the New Louvre.[5] The extension of the Palace of the Louvre in the 1850s to meet the emperor's residence in the Tuileries became the model for this architectural fashion.

The design of the New Louvre (Fig. 2) included several features that came to be considered standard ingredients for the Second Empire style. There is the use of pavilions, for instance, which mask the lack of parallelism between this wing and the older parts of the Louvre. The mansard roof is chosen, naturally enough, to harmonize with similar roofs on the Old Louvre and the Tuileries. Introduced in the 17th century, the mansard roof never totally disappeared from French architecture probably for practical reasons, since its particular form allows for maximum use of the attic space. At the New Louvre, however, the curved profile of the mansard roof introduced a new bombastic element that was unlike the more restrained 17th century type. This sculptural treatment of the roof was spiritually akin to the sumptuous classicizing decoration of the diverse façades.

Paradoxically, in spite of the international influence of the New Louvre, this monument had little impact on the public and domestic architecture of Paris. Except for the Grand Hotel and the Opéra, few public buildings reflected the compositional scheme or the sculptural richness of the New Louvre. The private residences and apartment houses erected following Napoleon III's code (uniformity of height, roofline and street alignment) showed Second Empire influence mainly in the use of the mansard roof; though the articulation of the façades often followed a grid-like pattern of horizontal and vertical divisions, the intermediate decoration, based on a play of classical motifs, rarely reflected the plasticity or three-dimensionality, usually associated with the Second Empire style (Fig. 3).

To understand why the Second Empire style made more impact in other countries than it did in France itself, it may be useful to consider the context from which these buildings emerged. The international renown enjoyed by Paris and the lavishness of the emperor's court were perhaps best exemplified in the Louvre project. This grandiose undertaking appealed to a very particular and socially conscious audience, for the New Louvre, after all, was grafted onto a building that for centuries had symbolized the glory of French monarchs. It is probably these courtly associations rather than the number of Parisian buildings in the Second Empire mode that explain why the reign of Napoleon III gave birth to an architectural style.

England: Early Advocate of Second Empire

The emergence of the Second Empire style in England occurred almost simultaneously with its appearance in Paris. It was used for buildings of such importance that it soon gained wide publicity and official support.

In 1852, the very year that Napoleon III was proclaimed emperor, the Great Western Railway Company completed the construction of Paddington Station and Hotel (Fig. 4) in London, a gigantic structure that anticipated in several ways the Second Empire style.[1] Indeed, a writer in the *Illustrated London News* of 1852 noted that this monument inaugurated the "French of Louis XIV or later" style.[2] Pavilions and mansarded towers were already part of the design, but they were less organically integrated into the mass than in later compositions of this type. On the other hand, the various façades, though soberly decorated, already showed an attempt to achieve plastic effects in the play of light and shadow. Because of its grandiose format and the high quality of its service, the Great Western Hotel at Paddington Station gained wide publicity.

This project was certainly not the only one to launch Second Empire fashion in England. In 1857, only five years after the New Louvre was begun, the British government held architectural competitions for the War Office and the Foreign Office. The two winning designs, those of Henry B. Garling for the War Office (Fig. 5), and Coe and Hofland for the Foreign Office, were both in the Second Empire style, proving to what point this fashion had already invaded the British architectural milieu. A tacit recognition of England's role in disseminating the style may be found in some remarks made in 1866 by the building committee for Boston City Hall:

A striking proof of this tendency [toward the Renaissance] is to be found in the fact that besides being long naturalized in France, and being the only style in which all the great works of improvement of modern Paris are composed, it has been so recognized and studied elsewhere, that in the great English competition for the projected new Government buildings, at Whitehall, the designs to which all the highest premiums (£800 each) were awarded, by a commission consisting of the most accomplished judges in the kingdom, were without exception in this style only.[3]

The publicity surrounding the Whitehall competition drew public attention to the Second Empire style and enhanced its popularity in England and, by extension, in North America.

Second Empire and the United States

For more than a decade, the Second Empire style enjoyed widespread popularity in the United States before disappearing as suddenly as it had emerged. During its popularity its presence was felt with equal force in both the public sector and the private domain.

The earliest significant public building to be designed in this style was Boston City Hall (Fig. 6), begun in 1862. The Committee on Public Buildings strove consciously to imitate French prototypes, even if such a move were controversial.

The style in which this building has been erected is so great an innovation on the character of our previously existing public structures as to have excited considerable attention, and to have called forth more or less of criticism and remark. It may be described as the Italian Renaissance, modified and elaborated by the taste of the French architects of the last thirty years.[1]

Though Boston City Hall was the first public building in this style in North America, the meteoric rise of Second Empire in the public domain was the result of its association with the central government in the reconstruction era following the Civil War; it became the official style of General Grant's administration (1869–77). Indeed, the style has been referred to in the United States as the "General Grant" style.[2] These flamboyant mansarded designs, incidentally, stood out in sharp contrast to earlier American public buildings of an austere classicizing style. Leading the government designers was Alfred B. Mullett (1834–90) who, in his role as supervising architect of the Treasury Department, was instrumental in popularizing the Second Empire style through the host of structures erected across the country by the new central administration.[3] One of his major extant works is the State, War and Navy Department Office Building in Washington (Fig. 7). For the public, Mullett's Second Empire structures came to symbolize the strength and power of the new central government.

Influence of the Second Empire style also reached the domestic scene where the introduction of the French or mansard roof stemmed from practical rather than symbolic considerations. The waxing and waning of the mansard roof's popularity in domestic buildings can be pinpointed through the so-called pattern books. They consisted of collections of house designs, with architectural details and plans, aimed at the growing middle class which wanted to erect well-designed homes but was unable to afford the luxury of custom-made architectural designs. Pattern books offered a range of sizes and styles to meet a variety of budgets.

The wide distribution of these pattern books was instrumental in establishing and disseminating canons of taste to the general public.

Designs for French-roofed cottages and residences began to appear in the pattern books in the early 1860s, peaked in the 1870s and disappeared by the early 1880s. The first ones took pains to underline the practical advantages of this new roof form. Writing in 1857, Calvert Vaux advised that "curved roofs especially deserve to be introduced more frequently than has hitherto been the practice here."[4] Remarking on the utility of mansard roofs, he noted,

Many to whom I have explained the principle of arrangement by an actual visit to executed houses, have expressed their surprise at finding a large, nearly level space, on the top of a house that showed no sign of any thing of the sort to a passer-by[5] *(Fig. 8).*

A few years later, another pattern book encouraged the use of the mansard roof also on practical grounds.

The French chateau roof, which we have adopted, gives ample space for servants' apartments and other necessary rooms in the attic, and, by the flat on top, furnishes a means of collecting water for the tank, and provides a place on which to walk, surrounded as it is, with an iron railing for protection.[6]

Besides the practical considerations, the question of fashion arises and the role that women played in the acceptance of mansarded designs. An American publication like *Godey's Lady's Book*, which presented a model cottage or villa in each issue, claimed a readership of 500,000 in 1869.[7] Between 1868 and 1875, the majority of house designs illustrated in this periodical drew on the Second Empire style (Fig. 9). The architect responsible for most of the designs in *Godey's Lady's Book*, Isaac Hobbs, republished them in a pattern book of 1873 in which at least half the designs have French roofs. Recognizing the influence of women in matters of architectural taste, Hobbs dedicated his volume "to the many ladies throughout the United States who have for years aided us by their suggestions in preparing many of the most practicable and beautiful ground plans found in this volume."[8]

While authors of pattern books usually offered a choice of styles, such as Italianate or Gothic, some deserve to be singled out as strong supporters of Second Empire designs; Gilbert B.

Croff, Marcus F. Cummings, Isaac Hobbs and George E. Woodward.[9] By 1880, however, American pattern books shifted focus and even these writers virtually eliminated mansard-roofed designs from their repertoire.

Both public and domestic architecture in the United States reflected a strong Second Empire influence in the third quarter of the 19th century. The economic and cultural interaction between the United States and Canada at this time was such that the impact of this influence on Canadian architecture cannot be underestimated.

Canada: Stirrings of Second Empire

Although Second Empire did not gain wide popularity in Canada before 1870, there were occasional hints of its impending ascendancy before that date. The mansard roof, of course, had been used for public and domestic buildings in New France, a direct import from 17th century France. However, mansard roofs were outlawed during the French regime because their massive structural components were considered to increase the hazard of fire. The earliest reappearance of the mansard roof, combined with other Second Empire features, seems to have been the design for the Toronto General Hospital. It was available to the general public, for a drawing by architect William Hay was published in the Toronto-based *Anglo-American Magazine* in 1854 (Fig. 10). It is interesting to note that Hay, Scottish-born and English-trained, had as his apprentice Henry Langley who later became one of the major proponents of Second Empire design in Ontario.

Another early example of the appearance of Second Empire features may be found in the winning designs of 1859 for government buildings to be erected at Ottawa for the Province of Canada. Although two different architectural firms participated in this grandiose project, the group of buildings presented a remarkably homogeneous appearance (Figs. 11, 12, 13). Three imposing buildings were arranged in stately U formation on the spectacular site known as Barrack Hill. There is no doubt that the basic concept comes from the Gothic Revival style. The original proposal submitted by Fuller and Jones, architects for the centre block, supported the use of the Gothic style for, as they explained, they "were fully convinced that a Gothic building only could be adapted to a site at once so picturesque and so grand."[1] And certainly much about the building is Gothic, including the rough masonry, pointed openings and round buttressed library resembling a mediaeval chapter house.

Other aspects of the design, however, are more closely allied to the Second Empire style. The mansarded towers with their flurry of iron cresting, for example, are drawn from Second Empire prototypes and contribute to the picturesque effect of the roofline. The Wellington Street façade is organized in balanced pavilion units so much in the spirit of Second Empire planning. This arrangement stems from the architects' assessment of the site. While acknowledging that the Gothic idiom was most appropriate for the rugged river side, Fuller and Jones believed that the more park-like nature of the Wellington Street frontage necessitated greater uniformity. Their solution for this façade, using symmetrical pavilions crowned by slate-covered mansard roofs, indicates their determination to create "a dignified, elegant, and also cheerful appearance, and that its character should tend more to the Palatial than the Castellated."[2] The undeniable importance of this undertaking, which attracted the attention of the entire architectural community and the Canadian public at large, meant that it had a significant influence on subsequent building in Canada.

Nevertheless, one of the first full-blown examples of Second Empire design in Canada appeared in Toronto in 1868 when the provincial authorities selected a Second Empire design for Government House, the official residence of the lieutenant-governor, that required a state dining room, ballroom and conservatory (Fig. 14). The architect was none other than Langley, previously mentioned in reference to the Toronto General Hospital. The public was made aware of the originality of this residence, for the *Canadian Illustrated News* reported that it was "in the modern French style of architecture."[3] With this building, one could say that the Second Empire style was truly launched in Canada. The fact that this was the residence of the provincial head of state and the centre of Toronto society in a sense put the official seal of approval on this new fashion. In Toronto its impact was immediately felt as is evidenced by the numerous "French style" mansions which appeared in the early 1870s in the fashionable residential suburbs.

For the architect, Henry Langley, this commission would have established his reputation within this stylistic idiom, and therefore it is not surprising that in 1871 the prestigious government contract of the new Toronto Post Office should have come his way.

Department of Public Works

To discover how the Second Empire style spread so rapidly across Canada, one must look in part at the Federal Department of Public Works. Like the United States, where the Second Empire or General Grant style was used often by the post-Civil War government, the new Dominion of Canada erected a series of imposing public buildings in this same mode. There is a striking difference between the buildings inherited by the Department of Public Works from the pre-Confederation era and those put up by the Dominion Government. The former were for the most part dependent on austere classicizing sources, while the early buildings of the new Canadian government drew without exception on Second Empire prototypes.

Immediately after Confederation, the Dominion Government launched a major building programme, especially for post offices and custom houses, to establish the federal image and provide necessary services in different communities. Actual construction was the responsibility of the Department of Public Works. Although a change of direction was evident from the outset of the building programme even while it was still administered by the incumbent F.P. Rubidge, assistant engineer from 1841 to 1872, the driving force was his successor T.S. Scott, appointed chief architect in 1872. The Second Empire vogue for federal buildings began before and continued throughout Scott's tenure with the Department of Public Works from 1872 to 1881.

The question arises as to who was the actual designer of any particular federal building. We know that local architects were involved in almost all the structures erected across Canada, which would suggest that each design should be different. Yet the striking similarity of these buildings indicates that some design control must have been exercised by Chief Architect Scott in Ottawa.

The interaction between the local architect and the chief architect can perhaps most easily be defined by examining a particular example, the Custom House in Saint John, New Brunswick (Fig. 15). The Department of Public Works sent written instructions to local architects McKean and Fairweather that included sketches of ground plans showing the size and arrangement of rooms and requirements for fireproofing. Scott had apparently attempted to find solutions to the problem of fire and insisted that certain measures like solid brick inner walls and wrought-iron roof framing be adopted. The choice of material for the exterior walls was left to McKean and Fairweather. Their proposal for grey and red granite, however, was overruled in Ottawa because Mr. Mackenzie, then prime minister, was "of opinion that it was, of all kinds of stone, the most liable to damage from fire."[1] Other changes made to McKean and Fairweather's design by the Department of Public Works, bringing it in line with other federal buildings, included the addition of mansarded towers and an increase in ornamentation.

Local architects did, however, have some influence on the final outcome; although Scott preferred brick for the Water Street façade, McKean and Fairweather argued successfully for stone on the grounds that, viewed from the harbour, it was actually the principal front of the Custom House. A contemporary observer summarized the relationship between McKean and Fairweather and the Department of Public Works when he praised "the great care of the architects ... in preparing plans and specifications, and in the supervision of the work during its progress. The building itself will stand as a monument to their taste and that of the Chief Architect and the Government".[2]

While federal buildings differed in scale and ornamentation depending on their location, the following selection built during Scott's tenure illustrates how similar they are to one another (Figs. 16–27). Standard features include stone as construction material (more permanent and prestigious); mansard roof with slate tiles arranged in decorative patterns on the slopes; pavilion massing with mansarded towers above (convex towers often over the central pavilions of larger buildings); classicizing sculptural decoration including quoins, carved keystones, string courses, pilasters and attached columns; picturesque roof effects like iron cresting, flagpoles, clocks and oval dormer windows. These characteristics are all part of the Second Empire mode as previously defined in reference to Montreal City Hall (Fig. 1).

The element of planning, another aspect of Second Empire, is also apparent in these designs. If we return to the example of the Custom House at Saint John, New Brunswick (Fig. 15), we discover that the exterior arrangement of the façade into central and side pavilions corresponds to the internal layout. There are in fact three distinct functions within the building, each one physically shut off from the others by interior walls of brick; the Custom House in the central section, the Inland Revenue Department and Board of Works in the north wing, and the Marine and Fisheries Department in the south wing.

These federal structures were intended to impress upon the observer the stability, permanence and wealth of the new nation. As symbols of the Dominion Government, most of them now demolished, they played an important role in the dissemination of the Second Empire style in Canada. With the replacement of Scott as chief architect in 1881, the style changed and evolved for Department of Public Works' buildings until it became an entirely different form.

Other Public Buildings

The choice of Second Empire for public architecture was not restricted to federal buildings; provincial and local governments as well as institutions and associations were quick to adopt this style for new structures erected under their jurisdiction.

Provincial governments chose Second Empire designs when circumstances required construction of new legislative buildings. Parliament House in Manitoba (Fig. 28), a Second Empire structure, had in fact been erected by the federal government, but it was provincial authorities in Quebec and New Brunswick that chose versions of Second Empire in the 1870s for their legislatures (Figs. 29–30).

The provinces also found the style acceptable for judicial buildings, as witnessed by the Law Courts Building in Charlottetown (Fig. 31) and the Court House in Winnipeg (Fig. 32). We have already observed that provincial authorities in Ontario selected a Second Empire design for the residence of the lieutenant-governor (Fig. 14).

Buildings that came under the jurisdiction of local governments, such as city halls and market halls, were not exempt from Second Empire fever in the 1870s, as examples like Montreal City Hall (Fig. 1), Victoria City Hall (Fig. 33), the Saint John Market (Fig. 34) and the Byward Market in Ottawa (Fig. 35) confirm.

Given government allegiance to the appropriateness of this style for public buildings, it is not surprising that other institutions followed suit. Ranging from asylums, such as Falconwood near Charlottetown (Fig. 36), to community halls, like the Athenaeum in St. John's (Fig. 37) and the Masonic Temple in Victoria (Fig. 38), these institutional buildings adopted the current fashion for exuberant mansarded designs. One organization that embarked on a major building programme in the 1870s was the Young Men's Christian Association (Y.M.C.A.). Although individual chapters hired local architects to design their multi-purpose structures, a common denominator of Y.M.C.A. buildings of this period put up at Toronto, Brantford, Montreal and Quebec City (this last one being the lone survivor) is their dependence on the Second Empire mode (Figs. 39–40).

Schools of course were no exception to this fashion. Since cost was a significant factor in most cases, the façades were often plain, although such features as the mansard roof and pavilion massing were retained. There appears to have been a difference between secular and Roman Catholic schools in terms of design. The secular examples are more individual and draw more directly on Second Empire prototypes, as the example in Truro, Nova Scotia (Fig. 41), suggests.

The Roman Catholic church, however, had a more far-reaching influence in the dissemination and perpetuation of at least the mansard roof. Many of the teaching orders put up parent buildings in the province of Quebec, large institutions with mansard roofs, pavilions and plain façades. An early and significant event was the "mansardization" of the main building of Laval University in Quebec City (Fig. 42). Founded in the mid-19th century under the auspices of the Seminary of Quebec, the university immediately erected the Central Pavilion, an enormous and austere flat-roofed block in keeping with the classicizing spirit of the day. Yet only 20 years later it was deemed appropriate to update the building by adding the splendid mansard roof which has become a Quebec City landmark. The undeniable stature of Laval University as an adjunct of the Seminary of Quebec meant that the mansard roof in a sense received official approval from the Roman Catholic establishment.

Whether or not the influence came directly from this example, it remains clear that schools, academies and teaching convents built by the Roman Catholic community in the last quarter of the 19th century adopted the mansard roof again and again (Figs. 43–44). Perhaps the fact that the mansard offered an additional living storey for dormitories encouraged its use by such institutions. This phenomenon was not limited to the province of Quebec: religious communities established missions in frontier areas, often in western Canada (Figs. 45–46). Long after the style became unfashionable, the church continued to put up massive mansarded institutions that came almost to symbolize culture, order and the Roman Catholic presence in the newly settled areas.

Commercial Building

The frequent use of Second Empire for public and institutional buildings implied that it could embody or symbolize such intangible values as permanence, stability, wealth, dignity, power – all attributes eagerly sought by the commercial sector. It is therefore hardly surprising that commercial enterprises in the 1870s chose this style for their structures.

The symbolic associations of the style may have been of particular value to the bankers of this country who faced faltering public confidence as a result of the economic depression of 1873. Second Empire was certainly their preferred choice in the 1870s. That bankers themselves were conscious of the link between architectural design and public confidence is aptly illustrated by a contemporary advertisement for the Jacques Cartier Bank in Montreal, a lavish building designed by Perrault. "These are institutions which prove both by their dividends and their palatial structures the vitality of Canadian commerce."[1]

In some instances this was not an idle boast, for such buildings as the Molson Bank in Montreal (Fig. 47) and the Dominion Bank in Toronto (Fig. 48) were indeed palatial. Others were less ornate, like the row of banks that occupied prime sites on Wellington Street in Ottawa across from the Parliament Buildings (Fig. 49). Here, soon after Confederation, several banking firms erected handsome buildings in the Second Empire style: the Bank of Quebec, the Bank of Ottawa, the National Bank, the Canadian Bank of Commerce and the Bank of Montreal. Together, they formed an imposing architectural ensemble, resembling one another in their height, scale, Italian repertoire and, of course, their mansard roofs. As a group, these banks once served as an attractive complement to the dignified public buildings across the street. By contrast, the structures erected by the Eastern Townships Bank are more subdued in character (Fig. 50–51). While they have mansard roofs with a suggestion of central pavilions and certain Italianate features such as semicircular windows, the overall treatment is restrained, far from the exuberance of the full-blown Second Empire style.

Like bankers, businessmen who put up multi-purpose commercial buildings to contain shops, offices and apartments had to contend with the high cost of property in the urban core. This consideration meant that land had to be exploited to its full extent. In practical terms, buildings had to come right out to the street frontage, so that valuable space would not be lost through wasteful pavilions. Consequently, commercial blocks in the Second Empire style – unlike public buildings – rarely have projecting and recessed wall planes. The suggestion of pavilion massing is restricted to the mansarded towers at roof level (Figs. 52–53).

When grouped together along major thoroughfares in large cities such as Montreal, these tall blocks with rich façades and ornate roofs offered a magnificent and imposing streetscape to the passerby (Fig. 54). The enormous corner building in this street view, known as Barron Block, illustrates another feature of this type, namely the corner entrance. The breadth of these immense buildings, often occupying entire municipal blocks, required at least two principal façades and special treatment of the rounded corners (Fig. 55). On a smaller scale, these blocks mushroomed in developing urban centres in Quebec and Ontario (Figs. 56–58) and with marked frequency in Winnipeg where the rise of Second Empire popularity coincided with the initial phases of that city's development (Fig. 59).

The early use of Second Empire for railway hotels in England has already been observed (Fig. 4). In Canada at least one first class hotel was designed in this style, the Windsor Hotel in Montreal (Fig. 60). A mark of the prestige of this luxurious hostelry is the fact that Lord and Lady Dufferin were among the guests who attended the gala inaugural festivities. While in no way matching the scale and significance of the Windsor Hotel, other smaller hotels built in Canada at this time often had mansard roofs and sometimes featured other traits of the Second Empire style (Figs. 61–62).

The use of this elaborate style extended even to utilitarian buildings like railway stations, warehouses and factories. The North Street Terminal in Halifax is surely one of the most palatial stations ever designed in Canada (Fig. 63). The fancy appearance of such a building as the Organ Factory of W. Bell & Company in Guelph (Fig. 64) belies its internal function. While the façade of the Guelph factory is articulated by a simple grid system, the roof is alive with clock tower, flagpoles, cresting and coloured slate tiles. In contrast to this flamboyance, the Chinic warehouse in Quebec (Fig. 65) is a conservative design, reflecting the influence of the Second Empire mode only in the mansard roof.

Although its period of glory was perhaps short-lived, Second Empire touched almost every aspect of commercial building in Canada, from banks and office blocks to hotels, stations and warehouses. Its widespread use in this area undoubtedly contributed to its popularity on the domestic scene.

Second Empire for Canadian Houses

To explain why in the late 1870s Second Empire suddenly became fashionable for domestic building, one automatically encounters the difficult problem of documenting popular taste. It would be facile to contribute this rising popularity to the influence of American pattern books discussed earlier. Although the connection is obviously valid, as is witnessed by a New York State pattern book which published a design for a Second Empire villa to be erected in Montreal (Fig. 66), access to such specialized publications was probably limited. On the other hand, weekly magazines like the *Canadian Illustrated News* and its French counterpart *L'Opinion publique* appealed to a more generalized readership. Published from 1869 to 1883, these magazines usually illustrated newly erected buildings in Canadian cities, many of which drew on the Second Empire style. It is interesting to compare the *Canadian Illustrated News*, directed toward a fashion-conscious urban readership, with Canadian periodicals aimed at the rural population, such as the *Canada Farmer* and the *Farmer's Advocate*. The latter invariably presented house types of austere simplicity, with no hint of Second Empire detail.

Although American pattern books and Canadian publications like the *Canadian Illustrated News* certainly helped to develop a taste for Second Empire, the physical presence of public and commercial buildings in this new style undoubtedly played a significant role in popularizing the fashion. The intangible qualities embodied by these large structures, such as stability, wealth, progress, power, and so forth, were desirable associations for aspiring gentlemen.

How is one to characterize the influence of Second Empire in Canadian houses? Perhaps the keyword is moderation. It is rare to find in the domestic sphere the sumptuous detail used in high-style public buildings. Reference to Second Empire sources is often manifested by the use of the mansard roof and vaguely Italianate details, which become vaguer as one moves away from the sophisticated urban centres. In its most simple form, the influence is reduced to the use of the mansard roof on otherwise plain structures or on dwellings whose main stylistic roots lie elsewhere.

The computerized information of the Canadian Inventory of Historic Building has proved invaluable in plotting certain general trends in domestic architecture. It has, for example, confirmed the hypothesis that this style is essentially urban; most Second Empire buildings recorded by the Canadian Inventory of Historic Building are located in cities and towns. Moreover, the computer has allowed us to trace regional variations that inevitably occur when a high style encounters local building traditions. For example, computer printouts readily verify that the predominant construction material changes from region to region; wood in the Atlantic Provinces, stone in Quebec, and brick in Ontario and Manitoba.

The geographical distribution is another element that emerges from an examination of the printouts. Buildings with Second Empire influence are numerous in the Atlantic Provinces, Quebec, Ontario and Winnipeg, but become extremely scarce west of Winnipeg. In spite of an early impression, based on preliminary research, that Second Empire influence was weak in Quebec and strong in Ontario, the cross-Canada printout of approximately four thousand residential buildings with Second Empire influence indicated that over half of these dwellings were in Quebec and less than one quarter were in Ontario. While this anomaly is partially attributable to sample size, the explanation rests primarily with the question of interpretation of "Second Empire influence." For the purpose of this study, the interpretation was made deliberately broad, in order to trace the influence to its ultimate vernacular expression. Hence, the many plain mansard-roofed cottages that dot the shores of the Saint Lawrence River inflate the number of Second Empire buildings in Quebec; on the other hand, though smaller in numbers, the Ontario examples are generally more elaborate in design and depend more directly on Second Empire prototypes.

In examining domestic architecture region by region, we have attempted to choose representatives or typical examples to reflect the variety found in the survey of the Canadian Inventory of Historic Building. That some of the simpler examples are not outstanding in terms of design may surprise the reader. Yet they represent the majority of houses recorded by the Canadian Inventory of Historic Building and may perhaps be considered a fairer reflection of the influence of Second Empire style as manifested at the vernacular or popular level.

Ontario Houses

For domestic buildings in Ontario, the Second Empire style assumed a variety of forms. The classic type is the free-standing residence, two storeys in height with an additional storey tucked into a ponderous mansard roof (Figs. 67–68). Most of these houses are built of brick, more often of yellow brick than of red. They pay tribute to the Second Empire idiom in their frequent use of round-headed doors and windows, pronounced eaves brackets, slate roof tiles arranged in decorative patterns, iron cresting atop weighty mansard roofs, and ornate dormer windows. The sophisticated design of many of these dwellings suggests close ties with models presented in American pattern books.

The most dignified examples of this type imitate the symmetrical arrangement of the façade found in public buildings in this style (Figs. 69–70). At the same time, however, a less formal version emerged which allowed for an asymmetrical massing of the façade (Figs. 71–73). Whether arranged symmetrically or asymmetrically, they generally attain a good deal of plasticity from bay windows that are sometimes carried up into the roof in tower-like forms.

Examples of this type still survive in what were developing urban centres in the 1870s – Toronto, London, Belleville, Brockville, Cobourg, Woodstock, Dundas, Port Hope, Brantford, Chatham, St. Catharines. A distinct regional variation occurs in the Galt-Guelph area where local custom called for stone instead of brick (Fig. 74).

A characteristic feature of Second Empire houses in Ontario is their massive bulk. Even when they are one storey high, they manage to attain a quality of weight and solidity (Figs. 75–76). Indeed, the impression can be one of top-heaviness with the mansard roof taking on visual importance disproportionate to the size of the house (Fig. 77).

While most Second Empire residential construction in Ontario occurs in attractively sited detached dwellings, the style is occasionally used for multi-purpose housing in the crowded urban core. The high cost of land meant that building lots were expensive; this necessitated the design of terraces (Fig. 78), row houses (Fig. 79) or narrow detached houses with plain side walls (Fig. 80) that would use the land economically. As one would expect, ornate Second Empire details are scaled down, but the mansard roof and sometimes even pavilion massing are retained.

The Canadian Inventory of Historic Building has recorded many fine examples of Second Empire houses in Ontario. The sophistication and careful execution of their details rank these houses among the purest high style examples in Canada. With their massive proportions and elaborate designs, they are the embodiment of the dignified and enduring family home.

Houses in the Atlantic Provinces

In the Atlantic provinces, Second Empire seems to have been welcomed with enthusiasm, judging from the houses recorded by the Canadian Inventory of Historic Building. In contrast to the solid massive dwellings in Ontario, builders in the Atlantic provinces instinctively grasped the picturesque quality of the style and interpreted it with a whimsy that one rarely finds elsewhere in Canada.

From the beginning of settlement in the Atlantic provinces there had been a marked preference for wooden structures: the Second Empire phase is no exception. Most houses are built of frame, with an exterior covering of clapboarding. More significant for the particular character of the buildings is the wealth of surface detail, so familiar to Maritime carpenters who grew up in a vernacular tradition that favoured abundant carved woodwork. Hence door and window surrounds teem with well-turned ornamentation; cornices are rarely left undecorated, with eaves enlivened by finely worked consoles, often grouped in pairs. The resultant play of light and shadow approximates the plastic effect achieved in carved stone on more formal Second Empire buildings (Figs. 81–82).

While wood was undoubtedly the prevalent building material in the Atlantic provinces, brick was used on rare occasions (Fig. 83). In the rebuilding after the great fire in Saint John, New Brunswick, there appeared a marked concentration of brick structures of Second Empire design. These residences, built of dark red brick, are distinguished by their elaborate details and by an angularity of form (Figs. 84–85).

What is distinctive about the interpretation of Second Empire details in the Atlantic provinces? One of the most obvious features is the well-ornamented three-sided or bay dormer window. These unusually large triple-paned dormers often borrow the round-headed windows and even the special oval windows from the Second Empire repertoire of forms. Used in conjunction with bay windows below, these bay dormers create an effect similar to the projecting pavilions of high-style Second Empire and contribute to the plasticity of the overall design (Figs. 86–89).

Another variation on the dormer window can also be isolated to the Maritimes. This is a window that cuts through the roof and reaches down to the wall. The resultant deep-set opening provides an opportunity to amass additional carved decoration in the form of giant consoles (Figs. 90–91).

True to Second Empire prototypes, the Atlantic provinces have their share of mansarded towers atop projecting central pavilions. While some examples occur on substantial sprawling villas (Figs. 92–93), others appear in a simplified form, especially in rural Newfoundland (Fig. 94). In the case of this modest vernacular version, the suggestion of a tower is reduced to an angular form akin to the cross-gable commonly found in the earlier classicizing tradition in the Atlantic provinces. With such a simplification of forms, one may well debate to what extent the flattened tower and central projecting section depend on Second Empire sources.

An examination of data from the Canadian Inventory of Historic Building reveals patterns of regional and local characteristics for the Atlantic provinces. In Saint John's, Newfoundland, for example, one frequently finds rows of two-storey clapboarded houses with almost flat front mansard roofs and gable dormers with inset round-headed windows (Fig. 95). Another popular Newfoundland feature is the semicircular dormer with a tidy eared moulding over the upper portion (Fig. 96). In Lunenburg, Nova Scotia, a number of houses have identical towers in which the projecting central pavilions display a variety of semicircular motifs for the door, sidelights, paired windows and slender windows on the side walls of the projection (Fig. 97). In Truro, Nova Scotia, on the other hand, all reference to round-headed forms is avoided in the shallow flattened bay windows two storeys high (Fig. 98).

As interpreted by builders of the Atlantic provinces, the Second Empire style assumes a lightness of form and distinctive decorative qualities not found in other parts of the country.

Quebec Houses

In Quebec the Second Empire style made a considerable impact although the high proportion of domestic buildings with Second Empire influence as indicated in the Canadian Inventory of Historic Building printouts is misleading. In order to trace the influence to its most vernacular form, the criteria of selection remain so broad that these printouts include many simple dwellings whose only reference to Second Empire sources is the mansard roof.

The revival of the mansard roof in Quebec in the 19th century is a curious phenomenon, one that is subject to varying interpretations. The mansard roof was well known in New France in the 17th and early 18th centuries; it had been used on grand public buildings like Frontenac's Château Saint-Louis and the Intendant's Palace as well as on simpler domestic structures. It disappeared from building practice in New France early in the 18th century and only reappeared in the third quarter of the 19th century.

The interpretation of the Second Empire style in Quebec depended on traditional building methods and materials already well established in the province. The purest examples, as previously noted, were concentrated in the major cities, especially in Montreal and Quebec. Whether for the mansions of the wealthy (Fig. 99) or for the multitude of terraces built at this time (Figs. 100–101), the skillful and varied use of stone masonry puts the stamp of Quebec on these houses. Nevertheless, brick masonry, being more economical than stone, was not excluded from row housing in less affluent quarters (Fig. 102).

These four examples, (Figs. 99–102), demonstrate a traditional Quebec feature that survived in the Second Empire style, namely the high basement wall and consequent raised ground storey. The elevated basement probably evolved in domestic architecture in Quebec as a result of heavy snow accumulations. Unlike examples in other provinces, the basement has in fact become a full living storey.

One of the features of the Second Empire style that apparently appealed to Quebec builders is the tower. Usually placed symmetrically in the main façade, it projects outward from the wall surface. At the same time, it is unusually tall and not well integrated into the composition; standing high above the roofline, it tends to create a rather elongated effect on the general massing (Figs. 103–105). Unlike examples in Ontario, where one finds a series of projections and recessions, the tower in the Quebec version is often the only interruption of the roof plane.

While high-style examples are rare in Quebec, the vernacular use of the mansard is a pervasive and enduring feature. It is applied to the typical Quebec rural house, one storey high, with the mansard replacing the traditional gable roof. A vestige of the earlier form may perhaps be found in the upper slope of the mansard roof which continues to have a marked pitch. Situated along the Saint Lawrence River, especially the Beaupré coast and the Island of Orleans, these wooden houses can appear with either the two-sided (Fig. 106) or four-sided mansard (Fig. 107). The influence even reached the so-called artisans' houses where the workshops are located on the ground level and the residential quarters above (Fig. 108).

Other more specific regional characteristics have emerged through the data of the Canadian Inventory of Historic Building. In the Eastern Townships, for example, one finds imposing two-storey brick residences, often with many details from the Second Empire repertoire, that are atypical in the Quebec context and akin to urban examples in Ontario (Fig. 109). On a different scale, the celebrated woodworking tradition of Saint-Jean-Port-Joli affects domestic buildings in this region, creating a series of richly decorated houses with an interplay of semicircular motifs (Fig. 110).

Although the pure forms of Second Empire did have an impact on the urban areas of Quebec, builders in rural Quebec frequently adopted only the most practical element of this style – the mansard roof. It was probably the practical advantage, and not the symbolic relationship to the mansard roof of the early French colony, that led to its frequent use in otherwise traditional Quebec houses.

Houses in the Prairies

In areas recorded by the Canadian Inventory of Historic Building, the full-blown Second Empire style seems to have made little impact on the Prairie provinces. This is not surprising if one considers that the early development of these regions occurred in the 1880s with the arrival of the railway, at a time when the popularity of the style was on the wane in central and eastern Canada. By the time settlers were able to build substantial dwellings, the Second Empire style had fallen from fashion.

The exception to this general statement is the city of Winnipeg which enjoyed a period of boom-town growth at the beginning of the 1880s. A significant number of houses built during this period followed the design principles of the Second Empire style. Although wall surfaces, almost invariably of yellow brick, were plain by eastern standards, details such as the tower feature and pavilion massing were derived from Second Empire prototypes (Figs. 111–112). On rare occasions, designs for residences of prominent citizens boasted an impressive scale and opulence of decoration comparable to similar houses in Ontario (Fig. 113).

Following the pattern established in other provinces, examples of Second Empire dwellings appeared in small developing towns along the main Canadian Pacific Railway line. In Manitoba, houses from this early phase of growth still survive in towns like Brandon (Fig. 114) and Emerson (Fig. 115). In spite of their obvious simplicity, such houses adopted certain Second Empire motifs like semicircular dormers and bay windows that contribute to the three-dimensionality of the effect. In Saskatchewan and Alberta, the Canadian Inventory of Historic Building found rare examples of this style, usually located in small communities along the railway line. These houses are frequently built of wood, the most readily available construction material in the area (Fig. 116); occasionally, however, stone is used, as in a fine example at Indian Head, Saskatchewan (Fig. 117).

With the exception of the city of Winnipeg, Second Empire influence in the Prairies was limited. The material of construction was typically brick in Manitoba, wood in Saskatchewan and Alberta. Though towers, mansard roofs and pavilion massing are often used, the designs are in general characterized by simplicity and austerity.

Houses in British Columbia

In British Columbia, the Second Empire style seems to have appeared only occasionally for residential building. Like the Prairies, development of this western province occurred in the latter years of the 19th century at a time when the vogue for Second Empire was already declining. As usual, houses of Second Empire design were concentrated in the urban centres, especially around the capital city of Victoria.

The presence of professional architects and the erection of several public buildings in this style may have encouraged the choice of this idiom for domestic building. Houses in Victoria (Fig. 118) and nearby Esquimalt (Fig. 119) indicate that local builders were well aware of Second Empire design principles even if, as in the case of Esquimalt, the interpretation remains individual.

Conclusions

The enthusiasm with which Second Empire was accepted in the 1870s is matched only by the rapidity with which it was rejected the following decade. The reasons for this change in fashion are difficult to isolate. The high cost involved in building such structures was clearly a contributing factor as was the notion that "Mansard roofed boxes" were foreign intrusions on the North American scene, "not adapted to our wants and times."[1]

One American writer, not hesitating to express his disdain, wrote that the New York Post Office "with its multiform and multitudinous roofs, and its banded sections of ugly, useless columns ... looked as though they were troubled with a continuous attack of influenza."[2] A more general assessment was made by comparing the roof form with a man's hat.

Give the dignified president [wearing a top hat] a smashing blow on the head and you see what he may become after an unsuccessful defalcation – an unfortunate tramp, who has 'seen better days'. He is a capital illustration of the roofs called 'French', that were so imposing a few years ago, and are about as agreeable in the way of landscape decoration as the tramp himself, but not half so picturesque.[3]

In spite of this inevitable reaction to so pronounced a style, Second Empire was nevertheless one of Canada's major architectural manifestations for almost two decades. In its most ornate phase, it affected all building types, but especially those of an official character – public buildings, institutions, banks – and the residences of the influential; in all cases, the desired effect was one of conservatism, stability, respectability and opulence.

Predictably, the style tended to be concentrated in fashion-conscious urban areas where the clientele had had the opportunity to develop more sophisticated tastes. Since the style reached the height of its popularity before the full expansion of western Canada, its major monuments are situated for the most part in Ontario, Quebec, the Atlantic provinces, and Winnipeg.

To judge from the buildings recorded by the Canadian Inventory of Historic Building, it is clear that Second Empire influences in a diluted form continued to be felt until at least the end of the 19th century. Indeed, some of the features associated with Second Empire resurfaced in the new context of other architectural styles.

Illustrations and Legends

1
City Hall
275 Notre Dame Street East, Montreal, Quebec
Constructed: 1872–78 (severely damaged by fire 1922, rebuilt)
Architect: H.M. Perrault
Material: Stone
With its mansard roof, pavilion massing, classicizing decoration
and fine setting, Montreal City Hall, described in detail in the text,
stands as a handsome early example of Second Empire design
in Canada.
(*Public Archives Canada*.)

2
New Louvre
Paris, France
Constructed: 1852–57
Architects: L.T.J. Visconti and Hector-Martin Lefuel
Material: Stone

The Louvre was begun in the 16th century by Pierre Lescot and continued by a succession of architects over the next 300 years. Napoleon III's decision to link up the Louvre with the Palace of the Tuileries required a design that would be compatible with the existing buildings. As a result the design of the new wing, which was conceived by Visconti and continued after his death in 1853 by Lefuel, borrowed many features from the older parts of the building such as the high-pitched mansard roof, horizontal emphasis and sculptural ornamentation; however, these forms were so vigorously interpreted that they created a robust and original architectural character.

Had this building been erected anywhere else but Paris, the design would probably not have had the same dramatic impact. The elegance of the court of Napoléon III and the ambitious urban planning schemes of Baron Haussmann had captured the imagination of the western world and earned the city its reputation as the model of cosmopolitan modernity. For the outside world the New Louvre became a symbol of this new progressive age.

(*Library of Congress*.)

3
Re-creation of a typical Paris apartment
Architects: Sanford E. Loring and William Le Baron Jenning
Published: 1869
This re-creation of a typical Paris apartment of the Second Empire period illustrates the type of buildings which lined the broad boulevards created by Baron Haussmann. They were usually six or seven storeys high with a shop and living quarters for the concierge on the ground floor and a *porte cochère* wide enough to admit a carriage into the narrow court leading to stables and carriage house at the rear. The first floor contained a graciously appointed apartment for a well-to-do tenant; each subsequent floor housed a series of progressively smaller and less elegant apartments ending with cramped garrets under the mansard roof. Individually the designs did not have the richness or plasticity of detail associated with the Second Empire style, but, when seen in conjunction with other similar buildings, an imposing streetscape was created. Haussmann's grand approach to urban planning provided a model for growing urban centres around the world.
(Sanford E. Loring, Principles and Practices of Architecture [Chicago, Cleveland: Cobb, Pritchard and Company, l869], ex. U, Pl. I.)

4
Paddington Station and Hotel
London, England
Constructed: 1852–53
Architects: Philip Hardwick and Philip Charles Hardwick
Material: Stone with cement sheathing
With the consolidation of the British railway system, the inferiority
of London terminal facilities became painfully evident and the
Great Western Railway Company's new hotel at Paddington, the
first of its scale, was intended to meet this need. Hailed as a
credit to the achievements of the age, it boasted 150 rooms and
aimed at providing every modern luxury and comfort for the
up-to-date tastes of prosperous travellers.
(*Royal Institute of British Architects*.)

5
Design for the War Office
Whitehall, London, England
Date: 1856–57
Architect: Henry B. Garling
Arranged around an interior courtyard, this building presented four monumental façades, each swarming with classical orders of great plasticity. Although never executed, the widely publicized plan provided a model for public building in the Second Empire style.
(*Royal Institute of British Architects*.)

6
City Hall
Boston, Massachusetts
Constructed: 1862–65
Architects: G.J.F. Bryant and Arthur D. Gilman
Material: Stone
By 1862 Boston had replaced Philadelphia as the artistic and intellectual centre of the United States; therefore, it is not surprising that the country's first monumental example of the Second Empire style should appear in that city. Boston City Hall's compact, rectangular plan and tightly knit façade may seem conservative when compared to the sprawling, complex layout of later Second Empire buildings such as Philadelphia City Hall and the State, War and Navy Department Building in Washington (Fig. 7). (*Historic American Buildings Survey*.)

7
State, War and Navy Department Building
Washington, D.C.
Constructed: 1871–87
Architect: Alfred B. Mullett
Material: Stone

Alfred B. Mullett's term as supervising architect to the Treasury Department (1866–74) covered a period of rapid government expansion. Of the many federal buildings designed by Mullett all but a few are in the Second Empire style; for this reason he has been justly regarded as the leading American exponent of this style.

The largest of these structures, the vast and imposing State, War and Navy Department Building, consists of a rusticated ground storey forming the base for the richly columned and pilastered tiers which are surmounted by a massive mansard roof. The exclusive use of the heavier, more powerful doric order was perhaps intended to reflect the military associations of the building. It was constructed of granite which had to be imported by rail from Richmond, Virginia. This extravagance partially explains an enormous construction cost of 12 million dollars. This was an era when government spared no expense to give its structures a suitable air of governmental authority and dignity. (*Historic American Buildings Survey.*)

8
Sketches of curved roofs
Designed: 1857
Architect: Calvert Vaux
Calvert Vaux's pattern book contains one of the earliest references to the potential picturesque effect inherent in the mansard or broken roof. These sketches of curved roofs, some of them mansards, may seem simple in comparison with later more bombastic examples, but they reveal Vaux's precocious awareness of the growing taste for the picturesque. In commenting on the sketches, he advised his readers that "some degree of picturesqueness can always be obtained by the treatment of the rooflines, or by the use of verandahs, porches, or baywindows; and these features, if well arranged, are very valuable in any case, for they help to supply the variety of light and shade which is so much needed. The introduction of circular-headed windows, circular projections or verandahs, and of curved lines in the design of the roof, and in the details generally, will always have an easy, agreeable effect, if well managed."
(*Calvert Vaux, Villas and Cottages* [*New York: Harper & Brothers, 1857*]*, p. 54.*)

9
French roof suburban villa for L.C. Thompson
Pottsville, Pennsylvania
Designed: 1877
Architect: Isaac H. Hobbs
This elevation for a Second Empire villa is one of many pattern book designs created by Philadelphia architect Isaac Hobbs and published in *Godey's Lady's Book*. Reacting to much modern building that he considered "outrageous trash", Hobbs insisted that good design must follow "a law of architectural proportion discovered by us ten years ago, which I have found unfailing in designing and executing work... . With it, the Mansard-roof ceases to be boxlike in appearance, and houses have the appearance of being worth twice or three times their cost." But Hobbs was not interested solely in aesthetics. He devoted his attention to practical details like ventilation, providing "in our drawings for air to pass between the rafters from apertures made in the planciers, which render French roofs very comfortable, they always having false ceilings, which leave space for ventilation above", and chimneys which "must be carried up above the house in order that no eddies of air blowing from any direction shall destroy their efficiency." Commenting on the success of his pattern book designs from both an aesthetic and practical point of view, Hobbs notes that "the intent ... is not only to assist those who may be about to build, but like the many works of the same character which have been published, to aid its readers in the cultivation of taste and the love of the beautiful, that they, too, may read 'sermons in stones'."
(*Godey's Lady's Book, Vol. 44, No. 561* [*March 1877*]*, p. 291.*)

10
Toronto General Hospital
Gerrard Street, Toronto, Ontario
Constructed: 1854–78 *Demolished*
Architect: William Hay
Material: Brick

At first glance, the design for the Toronto General Hospital has little about it that is Second Empire. The wall surfaces are exceedingly restrained, lacking the plasticity of the Second Empire style, and the sparse decorative features such as the pointed doorway with labels above are drawn from the Gothic Revival tradition. Nevertheless, the appearance of mansarded towers with their flurry of iron cresting and flags anticipates the development of full-blown Second Empire designs. The Scottish architect William Hay (1818–88) had ample opportunity to be aware of current European fashion for he had trained in the London office of G.G. Scott, acted as Scott's Clerk of Works for the Anglican cathedral in Saint John's, Newfoundland in the late 1840s, and returned briefly to Britain before setting up practice in Toronto in 1852. His innovative mansarded pavilions would have reached a wide public, for the proposal was published in the *Anglo-American Magazine*.

(*Anglo-American Magazine, Vol. 4* [*Jan.–June 1854*], *n.p.*)

11, 12, 13
Parliament Building and Departmental Buildings
Wellington Street, Ottawa, Ontario
Constructed: 1859–65 *Parliament Building demolished:* 1916
Architects: Thomas Fuller and Chilion Jones (Parliament Building); Thomas Stent and Augustus Laver (Departmental Buildings)
Material: Stone

Three imposing buildings were arranged in stately U formation on the spectacular site known as Barrack Hill. The measured, balanced arrangement of pavilions on the Wellington Street façade of the Parliament Building, and the individual mansarded towers are early manifestations of Second Empire design. The boldly picturesque effect of the roof, revealed in the 19th-century photograph from the rooftop of the western Departmental Building (Fig. 13), is created by the maze of ornamental chimneys, iron cresting, towers, and the decorative multi-coloured shingles (*Public Archives Canada*.)

12

14
Government House
King and Simcoe Streets, Toronto, Ontario
Constructed: 1868–70 *Demolished:* 1912
Architect: Henry Langley
Material: Brick
The lieutenant-governor's residence in Toronto is not only one of
the grandest examples of the Second Empire style in domestic
building but it is also one of the earliest manifestations of this new
fashion in Canada. Even at this early stage the Second Empire
vocabulary was fully developed. The mansard roof, the broken
wall planes, the contrasting colours of stone against brick, and
the picturesque roofline accented by the central tower with iron
cresting together create a highly animated design reflecting
the taste for richness and variety of forms.
(*Public Archives Canada.*)

15

Custom House

Prince William Street, Saint John, New Brunswick

Constructed: 1877–81 *Demolished:* 1961

Architects: Department of Public Works; J.T.C. McKean and G.E. Fairweather, supervising architects

Material: Stone

The Saint John Custom House is one of the largest Public Works' buildings to be designed in the Second Empire style. The fact that two of the three ministries to be housed in this building were at the time headed by New Brunswick representatives – the Honourable Isaac Burpee, Minister of Customs, and Sir Albert J. Smith, Minister of Marine and Fisheries – may have had some influence on the decision to build on such a massive scale. The local press, however, had no objection to this expensive monument and they proudly boasted that "it was probably the finest Custom House in America and second to very few in the world."

   Designed in what was referred to as a "free rendering of the Classical style," it is characterized by a play of convex and straight roof shapes, a favourite theme for Public Works' designs. Because of the unusual length of the façade two towers were added at each end to add visual strength to the corners. (*Public Archives Canada*.)

16

Custom House

Richmond Street, London, Ontario

Constructed: 1872–74 *Demolished*

Architect: Department of Public Works; William Robinson supervising architect

Material: Stone

Although the use of the mansard roof places this building within the Second Empire idiom, the design reflects a conservative trend toward the established classical styles. The façade composition, with its heavy rusticated basement pierced by simple round-headed windows, surmounted by a high, more elaborately articulated first floor and topped by a lower attic storey, is ultimately derived from the Italian Renaissance palazzo. Each architectural element is isolated against the flat wall surface imparting a sense of restraint and clear definition of parts, unlike the grand sweep of bombastic sculptural detail often found in Second Empire public buildings. Alterations to the Custom House include the removal of a central clock tower and the addition of a rear wing in 1885 by local architect, George F. Durand.

   William Robinson, the supervising architect of the Custom House, 1872–74, immigrated to Canada from Ireland in 1833, and opened an architect's office in London in the mid-1850s; in 1857 he was appointed city engineer. He held this position for 21 years while maintaining at the same time a successful private practice in surveying, civil engineering and architecture. (*Canadian Inventory of Historic Building*.)

16

17, 18
Post Office
Adelaide Street, Toronto, Ontario
Constructed: 1871–74 *Demolished:* 1960
Architect: Department of Public Works; Henry Langley, supervising architect
Material: Stone façade, brick sides

The Toronto Post Office marked the beginning of a ten-year reign of the Second Empire style in federal architecture. Its building history reveals that this change was not caused by the arrival of T.S. Scott in 1871 as chief architect, but by conscious government policy to create a new and more progressive public image through its buildings. Although Scott was responsible for orchestrating this massive programme of Second Empire building, the stylistic transition actually began prior to his appointment.

In March of 1870 John Dewe, Post Office Inspector for the Toronto Division, submitted a set of plans to chief architect, F.P. Rubidge, for the new Toronto Post Office which he described as "chaste, elegant and in perfect taste and highly creditable to Mr. Mullett, the architect by whom they have been drawn." Although these plans have disappeared one can be fairly certain that they featured the Second Empire style for their designer, Alfred B. Mullett, chief architect for the Treasury Department in Washington, was well known as the leading American exponent of this new fashion (Fig. 7). Mullett was never called upon to produce any further plans; instead, the commission was given to Henry Langley of Toronto who had already demonstrated his proficiency in this idiom with his design for the lieutenant-governor's residence in Toronto (Fig. 14). The drawing (Fig. 17) probably represents one of Langley's preliminary proposals which could date as early as 1870. In the final version, a pediment and coat of arms were added over the main entrance and the east wing was eliminated. It would appear from this early design that even in these pre-Scott days the taste for Second Empire was fully developed.

(Photograph: Public Archives Canada; drawing: Ottawa, Department of Public Works.)

17

19
Post Office
Elgin Street, Ottawa, Ontario
Constructed: 1872–76 *Demolished:* 1938
Architect: Department of Public Works; Walter Chesterton, supervising architect
Material: Stone

The favoured site for the new Post Office was located in what is today Confederation Square, directly across from the East Block of the Parliament Buildings. The objection was raised that a building in this location would injure the view of the Parliament Buildings; however, Chief Architect T.S. Scott felt "that the façade of the Post Office could be so made as to accord with, and be erected in the same style as 'public buildings'." While Chesterton's design obviously did not borrow any of the gothic detailing of the Parliament Buildings, the use of pavilions, towers, mansard roof and iron cresting is common to both designs, creating a unified skyline of a lively and picturesque nature. The unusual tower-like feature over the central pavilion of the Post Office is unique to the Department of Public Works' Second Empire designs and was probably intended to give a stronger vertical emphasis to further harmonize with the nearby Parliament Buildings.

(*Public Archives Canada.*)

20
Post Office
Saint James Street, Montreal, Quebec
Constructed: 1872–76 *Demolished*
Architect: Department of Public Works;
H.M. Perrault, supervising architect
Material: Stone

The Montreal Post Office was one of the finest examples of Second Empire to be found in Canada. Not only did it feature all the basic ingredients of high Second Empire style – mansard roof, pavilion massing, robust classical ornamentation and picturesque roofline – but it coordinated this profusion of detail into a tightly organized composition controlled by the massive corinthian columns and pilasters two storeys high. The ground floor was defined by short piers and columns which provided a sturdy base for the grand projecting portico above. This use of freestanding forms and the resulting effects of light and shade gave the façade its strong feeling of three-dimensionality and monumentality.

Situated on the prestigious Saint James Street, the heart of Montreal's financial and business community, the Post Office had to compete with nearby impressive buildings like the Bank of Montreal of 1848 by John Wells. The federal government, intent on making its presence felt, chose, for the Post Office, a prominent site and sumptuous manner that would equal or surpass its neighbours.
(*Public Archives Canada.*)

21
Custom House
Front and Yonge Streets, Toronto, Ontario
Constructed: 1873–76 *Demolished:* 1919
Architect: Department of Public Works; R.C. Windeyer, supervising architect
Material: Stone
The Toronto Custom House was one of the most unusual and
distinctive buildings to be erected by the federal government
under T.S. Scott's reign as chief architect. The full bulbous form
of the convex mansard roof, the bevelled corners and the free
interpretation of the classical detail together produced its unique
architectural character. The façade of the Toronto Custom House
was organized in the typical grid system of pilasters and entabla
tures; however, the intricate stone detail with carved heads, tall
ornamental pediment and decorative bands had an unusually
organic and baroque character. To modern taste this building
would perhaps seem overdone but at the time of its completion
this bombastic structure was well suited to Toronto's mood of sel
assurance. The city was extremely proud of this building and it
was described in glowing terms as "a palace not unworthy of the
commercial interests of a great and progressive city."
(*Public Archives Canada.*)

22
Post Office
Government Street, Victoria, British Columbia
Constructed: 1873–74 *Demolished*
Architect: Department of Public Works; Benjamin W. Pearse,
resident engineer
Material: Brick

The Victoria Post Office was the first federal building to be
erected in the newly confederated province of British Columbia.
Although the Department of Public Works was not generally
known for its frugality, in this case it seemed intent on keeping
the building costs down. Except for some modest flourishes
around the door and the quoining at the corners and windows the
design displays none of the refinement of detail usually found on
even the smallest of public buildings in the east. The functional
nature of the design was described by the architect, Benjamin
Pearse. "The building, though not aesthetically beautiful, is of a
very substantial character."

Benjamin W. Pearse had been employed as the Surveyor
General under the colonial government and in 1872 was hired by
the Department of Public Works as its resident engineer, a post
which he held for many years.
(*Public Archives Canada*.)

23
Custom House
1002 Wharf Street, Victoria, British Columbia
Constructed: 1873–75
Architect: Department of Public Works
Material: Brick

As originally planned all government offices in Victoria were to b
housed in the Post Office building (Fig. 22) but it soon became
apparent that a separate building would be required to accommodate the Custom House and the offices of the Departments c
Inland Revenue and Marine and Fisheries. In appearance the
Custom House resembles the Post Office, although the façade
has an even greater simplicity. While one cannot pretend that th
Custom House and Post Office were among the better achievements of the Department of Public Works, they nevertheless
had an important effect on local architecture – witness the group
of Second Empire buildings such as the Victoria City Hall (Fig.
33) built in Victoria in the late 1870s.
(*Canadian Inventory of Historic Building*.)

24
MacKenzie Building
Royal Military College, Kingston, Ontario
Constructed: 1876–78
Architect: Department of Public Works; Robert Gage, supervising architect
Material: Stone

The MacKenzie Building, named after Prime Minister Alexander MacKenzie, was built to house the administrative and educational functions of Canada's first military college which opened in 1876. The 1877 annual report of the chief architect (T.S. Scott) for the Department of Public Works describes the building as "plain in design and substantial in character. The outer walls are built of local limestone with cut stone quoins, plinth, strings and drawings to windows and doors; the stonework is supplied and cut at the Kingston Penitentiary." Consistent with federal building during Scott's term as chief architect the design is of the Second Empire style although not as grandly elaborate as his other large public buildings. Perhaps it was felt that more sober interpretation would better harmonize with the existing buildings on the square and at the same time give a fittingly military appearance to the structure.

(*Canadian Inventory of Historic Building.*)

25

Post Office, Custom House, Inland Revenue Building
Saint George Square, Guelph, Ontario
Constructed: 1876–78 *Demolished*
Architect: Department of Public Works
Material: Stone

As was often the case for smaller urban centres, the plans for this
building were prepared by Department of Public Works' staff in
Ottawa instead of being contracted to a local designer. Nevertheless, this absentee architect must have had a good understanding of the local architectural character in order to produce a
design which harmonized so successfully with its environment.
Except for the elaborate brackets under the small tower and
the ornate balcony over the main door, which together accent the
central entrance, the decoration is quite severe and restrained
by Department of Public Works' standards. The emphasis of the
design lies with the surface texture of local limestone masonry
whose sturdy quality is so characteristic of buildings in Guelph.
(*Public Archives Canada*.)

26
Architectural drawing of the Post Office, Custom House and Inland Revenue Building
Richelieu Street, Saint-Jean, Quebec
Constructed: 1877–80 *Demolished*
Date of Drawing: 1878
Architect: Department of Public Works
Material: Brick
The plans for the Saint-Jean Post Office were drawn up by Department of Public Works' staff in Ottawa with on-site supervision provided by the Montreal firm of architects, Alex C. Hutchison and A.D. Steele. Although these central office designs did not follow any standardized formula, the stamp of the Ottawa office can often be identified by several decorative motifs. For example, the near contemporary Guelph Post Office (Fig. 25), despite a difference in material and scale, shows the same central focus with raised tower, ornamental balcony over the main doorway, narrow doubled string courses which define the floor divisions and link the ground storey windows, and similar cornice motif with brackets interspaced by rectangular panels.
(*Ottawa, Department of Public Works.*)

27
Architectural drawing of the Post Office and Custom House
Pitt Street, Windsor, Ontario
Constructed: 1878–80 *Demolished*
Architect: Department of Public Works; William Scott, supervising architect
Material: Stone, two sides; brick, two sides
The façade composition of the Windsor Post Office and Custom House, with its central round-headed doorway, second floor balcony and slightly projecting pavilion form in the mansard roof is very similar to the design of both the Saint-Jean and Guelph federal buildings (Figs. 25, 26). Although the Windsor building was conceived by local architect-builder William Scott, the consistency of these motifs would suggest that the chief architect's office in Ottawa exercised considerable control over the final design. The Windsor Post Office and Custom House, however, is set apart from the typical Department of Public Works' design in its subtle gothicizing note created by the slightly pointed arches of the radiating voussoirs over the ground floor windows.
(*Ottawa, Department of Public Works.*)

27

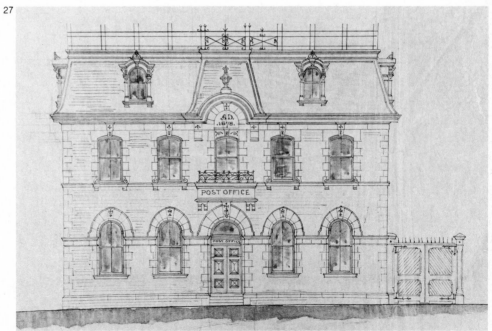

28
Parliament Building
Kennedy Street, Winnipeg, Manitoba
Constructed: 1881–83 *Demolished:* 1920
Architect: Department of Public Works; J.P.M. Lecourt, supervising architect
Material: Brick with stone trim

The erection of a permanent legislative assembly for the province of Manitoba became the responsibility of the federal government. The fact that the plans were prepared in Ottawa perhaps explains why the contractors for the building were the Ottawa-based firm of J. & P. Lyons & Company. The Parliament Building bears the standard trademarks of Department of Public Works' design at this time, including organisation of the façade into pavilion units and a variety of mansarded roofs and towers. The sessional papers state that "the style of architecture adopted is Italian, modified to suit the requirements of the climate." Although the Parliament Building does not have as much decoration as other governmental buildings in the Second Empire mode, it has a grace and dignity due in large measure to the rhythmic play of semicircular and segmental openings. In accordance with its primary function, the Parliament Building housed an impressive legislative chamber surrounded by galleries on three sides. It apparently met with local approbation as witnessed by one account which calls it "a handsome structure, and equal, if not superior, to any Provincial building in the Dominion."

The designer of the Parliament Building, J.P.M. Lecourt, began his career in Quebec City, moving to Ottawa in the mid-1860s to become staff architect for the Department of Public Works. For over a decade he monopolized Winnipeg's federal architecture after being transferred to this western city during the hectic building boom of the early 1880s.
(*Public Archives Canada.*)

29
Parliament Buildings
Dufferin Avenue, Quebec, Quebec
Constructed: 1877–87
Architect: Eugène Taché (exterior); Jean-Baptiste Delorme and
Pierre Gauvreau (interior planning and supervision)
Material: Stone
It would be tempting to ascribe the use of the Second Empire
style to an expression of French Quebec nationalism were it not
for the general popularity of this style in North America and the
strong similarities of Quebec's Parliament Building with other
public institutions in Canada. In many ways Taché's design
is really a classicized version of Fuller and Jones' central block
for the Parliament Buildings in Ottawa. This parallel is particularly
apparent in the main towers, both characterized by their tall
slender form and similar turret-like details called bartizans.
Nevertheless, Taché clearly meant to express a cultural link with
France. Like the Louvre in Paris, The Quebec Parliament Building
is composed of wings that enclose a central courtyard and the
practice of dedicating the pavilions to important historical figures
like Jacques Cartier, Champlain and Maisonneuve is borrowed
from its French counterpart.
(*Public Archives Canada.*)

30
Legislative Building
750 Queen Street, Fredericton, New Brunswick
Constructed: 1880–82
Architect: James C. Dumaresq
Material: Stone
The need for a new Legislative Building in New Brunswick was regarded as an opportunity to provide the province and the country with a fittingly grand architectural symbol to the province's spirit of self-confidence. These ambitions were well expressed in an article of 31 March 1880 in the *New Brunswick Reporter*: "We hope that the House will vote such an amount as will enable the Government to erect a structure that will not only adequately provide for both houses of the Legislature, Law Courts, Library, etc., but one that will be a credit in point of design, elegance and architecture to the province ... handsome as well as substantial, and commensurate with the progressing spirit of the age in which we are living." With these requirements in mind it is not surprising that James Dumaresq's winning design should be in the expensive and prestigious Second Empire style; however, elements such as the cupola and pedimented frontispiece reflect a conservative leaning toward the established classical styles which were so well entrenched in local architectural tradition.
(*Canadian Inventory of Historic Building*.)

31
Law Courts Building
171 Richmond Street, Charlottetown, Prince Edward Island
Constructed: 1874–76
Architect: Thomas Alley
Material: Brick

The Law Courts Building offers a simplified version of the Second Empire style in public building. Pavilions have been suggested in the four central towers but these forms are not continued below the eaves line. The cut stone trim and highly decorative brickwork under the eaves (features typical of Alley's work) add colour and texture to these surfaces but lack the full sculptural feel of high Second Empire detailing.

Despite its modest execution, this building achieved a sense of grandeur in the context of its site. Prominently situated on Queen's Square in the heart of Charlottetown, it stood next to the Provincial Building and was counter-balanced on the west side of the square by the Post Office. Together these three buildings created an imposing architectural ensemble that visually proclaimed their role as the core of provincial authority. Unfortunately the Post Office is no longer standing and the Law Courts Building was severely damaged by a fire in 1976.
(*Public Archives Canada.*)

32
Court House
Kennedy Street, Winnipeg, Manitoba
Constructed: 1882–83 *Destroyed by fire:* 1957
Architect: C. Osborn Wickenden
Material: Brick with stone trim

With the erection of the Winnipeg Court House, Second Empire burst upon this prairie town with a sophistication that could rival almost any building in eastern Canada. Though not large, it has strength and monumentality as a result of its harmonious proportions and careful detail. All the standard Second Empire features are used, including symmetrical massing, mansarded tower, superimposed orders, semicircular and round windows, and of course the rich sculptural texture of the façade. "Designed after the French Renaissance," according to one contemporary source, the Court House became a landmark because of its 80-foot tower, "the highest in the city and a conspicuous object for miles around."

To produce such a fashionable building, it is hardly surprising that provincial authorities called upon an architect and contractor of experience. Wickenden, trained as an architect in England, had worked in New York before emigrating to Saint John, N.B. after the 1877 fire. It was in Saint John that he met J.G. McDonald, contractor for several major buildings at the time. They may well have decided together to try their fortune in boom-town Winnipeg where they collaborated on the Court House.

Ranged along Kennedy Street beside two other Second Empire buildings, the Parliament Buildings (Fig. 28) and the Lieutenant-Governor's residence, the Winnipeg Court House contributed to an imposing streetscape that served as a fitting embodiment of the power and permanence of government. *(Provincial Archives of Manitoba.)*

33
Victoria City Hall
Centennial Square, Victoria, British Columbia
Constructed: 1878, 1881, 1890
Architect: John Teague
Material: Brick

John Teague, a native-born Englishman, settled in Victoria in 1858 and worked for a number of years as a contractor for the naval dockyards. In 1875 he set himself up as an architect and became the major local designer of the period. His most important work was the City Hall and, like many of his other public buildings, it was designed in his own particular version of the Second Empire style. It is interesting to compare Teague's building of 1878 with Perrault's Montreal City Hall (Fig. 1), just being completed that year, to demonstrate the widely differing interpretations possible within this idiom. In contrast to the heavy, plastic massing and detail of Perrault's design, the Victoria City Hall is more compact in plan and elevation, and has shallow detailing of a lighter and more two-dimensional character. In Victoria the style was labelled as either the "Italian" or "Anglo-Italian" style and in fact an Italian renaissance influence is evident in the round-headed windows with their circular tracery motif.

Although entirely designed by John Teague, the City Hall did not assume its final appearance until 1890. Because of financial difficulties only the south wing, defined by the three bays to the left, was erected in 1878. In 1881 the Fire Hall was added to the rear of the south wing and by 1890, the economy of Victoria having greatly improved, the main facade was extended by 82 feet along Douglas Street and the clock tower was added. (*Canadian Inventory of Historic Building.*)

34
City Market Building
47 Charlotte Street, Saint John, New Brunswick
Constructed: 1876
Architects: J.T.C. McKean and G.E. Fairweather
Material: Brick
This market building was preceded by two earlier structures, both of which were constructed of wood and later destroyed by fire. To prevent a third mishap the new market was constructed of brick, a worthwhile expenditure for it was one of the few buildings in the area to survive the fire of 1877. Similar in spatial organization to a railway station, the plan consists of a front block with an imposing entrance, office space and an actual market area housed in a long functional structure at the rear, well lit by a row of clerestorey windows. The façade articulation with its semicircular windows and corbelling under the eaves seems to be a favorite decorative combination for public buildings of the Second Empire style in the Maritimes. Comparable treatment of exterior design can be found on the Charlottetown Law Courts (Fig. 31) and the Public School at Truro (Fig. 41).
(*Canadian Inventory of Historic Building.*)

35
Byward Market Building
York Street, Ottawa, Ontario
Constructed: 1865–76
Architect: Robert Surtees?
Material: Brick
Following the lead of the federal government most Ottawa municipal buildings in the 1870s, including the City Hall of 1878 (demolished in 1931), were designed in the Second Empire styl Ottawa's Byward Market building, like the City Market building in Saint John, New Brunswick, of the same year, was planned with a long utilitarian market hall hidden behind a more style-conscious entrance block. It is a modestly detailed building but attractive for its gracefully flared mansard roof and central pavil ion topped by a delicate, jewel-like lantern. Although the documentation is not conclusive, the design was probably the work c city engineer, Robert Surtees.
(*Public Archives Canada.*)

36
Falconwood Lunatic Asylum
Charlottetown, Prince Edward Island
Constructed: 1877–78 *Demolished*
Architect: David Stirling
Material: Brick

In 1876 a competition was held for the design of the new Falcon-wood Lunatic Asylum. Eleven proposals were received and the contract was awarded to David Stirling of the Halifax firm of Stirling and Dewar. This firm had just completed a mansarded design for the Halifax Poor House in 1875 and it was perhaps this experience in institutional building that gave them an advantage over the other competitors.

The design reduced the Second Empire style to its most sim-ple geometric forms. All decorative details were stripped away, leaving a pavilioned plan of heavy broad masses which pivot around the central block and tower. This illustrates well the close interrelationship between form and planning in that each of the separate units was an outgrowth of interior function. The central block housed administrative services; day rooms and recreation halls were located in the pavilions, and the intervening spaces were occupied by dormitories. The above illustration does not represent the building as completed, since research indicates that only the west or left-hand wing and central block were erected in 1877. The east wing was built between 1896 and 1901 in a similar style but with modifications to the original plans.
(*L'Opinion publique* [*Montreal*], *23 mars 1878, p. 180.*)

37
The Athenaeum
Duckworth Street, St. John's, Newfoundland
Constructed: 1875–78 *Destroyed:* 1892
Architects: J. and J.T. Southcott
Material: Brick
In March 1861, the St. John's Library and Reading Room, Young
Men's Institute, Mechanic's Institute and Museum were amal-
gamated into the Athenaeum. Land was granted by the governo
for a building on Duckworth Street; however, construction did
not begin until 1875. The design was by the father and son firm o
J. and J.T. Southcott, leading local architects working primarily
in the Second Empire style who provided a key impetus in creating the immense popularity of this style in St. John's. The lively
exterior composition, which has been unified by the play of semi
circular and circular motifs of the door and window tracery and
surrounds, reveals the accomplished style of the Southcott family. This building was one of many lost in the fire of 1892.
(*Newfoundland Public Library Board*.)

38
Masonic Temple
650 Fisgard Street, Victoria, British Columbia
Constructed: 1878
Architect: John Teague
Material: Brick

Like the Y.M.C.A., the Order of Freemasons favoured the Second Empire style for their lodges during the 1870s. An example of this period of building is the Masonic Temple in Victoria, designed by the city's leading architect, John Teague, who was working primarily in the Second Empire style (*see* Fig. 33) and who, not surprisingly, was also a prominent member of the Masons. The construction contract was awarded to the firm of Dinsdale and Malcolm of Victoria. As originally constructed the building extended four bays along Douglas Street and three bays along Fisgard Street with a corner entrance accented in the roofline by a small tower. Shops occupied the ground floor and the lodge facilities were located on the second floor. In 1909 a large addition was built on the Fisgard Street façade and the original second-storey windows were bricked in giving the design, which was plain at the outset, its flat, lifeless appearance. (*Canadian Inventory of Historic Building*.)

39, 40
Young Men's Christian Association
950–964 Saint-Jean Street, Quebec, Quebec
Constructed: 1879
Architect: Joseph-Ferdinand Peachy
Material: Stone

The extant Y.M.C.A. building in Quebec has an asymmetrical plan, probably due to the exigencies of the building lot, but in other respects illustrates the major stylistic features of Second Empire. The contrasting colour and texture of the masonry, the fine detailing coordinated by rhythmic successions of structural openings, and the picturesque silhouette reflect the delight in rich surfaces and outline so characteristic of this style. The building initially housed four shops, a lecture hall, reading room, gymnasium and numerous apartments; however, all that remains of the once elegant interior is a grand staircase. Over the years, the exterior of the building has been sadly altered. The arcaded storefronts have been replaced by plate-glass windows and the roof has lost its patterned shingles, iron cresting and ornamental chimneys. In its present state, the Y.M.C.A. building in Quebec has a stolid and top heavy appearance far from its original inspiration.

(*Fig. 39, source unknown; Fig. 40, Canadian Inventory of Historic Building.*)

40

41
Provincial Normal School
748 Prince Street, Truro, Nova Scotia
Constructed: 1877–79
Architect: Henry F. Busch
Material: Brick

Like many educational institutions in Canada during the 1870s, the Provincial Normal School, erected by the Provincial Department of Education as a teachers' training centre, was designed in the Second Empire style. Features such as the balanced pavilion massing and the play of concave and convex forms in the mansard roof were drawn from the Second Empire vocabulary; however, unlike the heavy classical detail found in purer forms of this style, the façade is lightly articulated by contrasting patterns and colours of brickwork. This lively appearance is further enhanced by the repetition of semicircular and circular forms which unite the façade. As originally built the roofline was decorated with iron cresting and a small ornamental cupola over the central pavilion. The architect, Henry F. Busch of Halifax, seemed to be a favourite of the Department of Education for in 1878 he produced a very similar design for the Halifax County Academy on Brunswick Street in Halifax.
(*Engineering and Architecture, Department of Indian Affairs and Northern Development.*)

42

Pavillon central, Laval University
3–7 University Street, Quebec, Quebec
Constructed: 1854–56; addition 1875-76
Architects: Charles Baillairgé and Joseph Ferdinand Peachy
Material: Stone

Seen from the rear in this view, the main college building of Laval University is faithful to Baillairgé's design with the exception of the roof. Baillairgé's original conception for the structure called for a flat roof deck surrounded by an elaborate cast-iron balustrade. By the 1870s, this severely rectilinear design was apparently considered inappropriate, and the Seminary of Quebec engaged Peachy, a former apprentice of Baillairgé, to add the robust mansard roof. The round-headed dormers, iron cresting, central pavilion with lantern and side lanterns with weathercocks all contribute to the picturesque effect so dear to Second Empire ideals. The actual construction was carried out by master joiner Ferdinand de Varennes, a frequent collaborator with Peachy. Perched on the rock of Quebec overlooking the Saint Lawrence River, this gleaming metal-covered roof continues to be a prominent landmark of Old Quebec.

(*Canadian Inventory of Historic Building*.)

43

Collège du Sacré-Coeur
College Street, Sorel, Quebec
Constructed: 1877 *Demolished*
Architect: L.-Z. Gauthier
Material: Stone

The new college is an odd combination of traditional Quebec traits and fashionable Second Empire. The walls of evenly coursed rough-faced stone and the smooth cut-stone trim around doors and windows are common Quebec features. But the use of central and side pavilions, marked by cut-stone quoins, and the wonderfully flamboyant roof with convex central cupola and concave corner towers illustrate the inroads made by the new fashion. The architect of the Collège du Sacré-Coeur, L.-Z. Gauthier, later worked in Ottawa on a design for the western wing of the Archbishop's Palace. The construction of the college was supervised by Father Arthur St-Louis. The building's function as a classical college was short-lived, for the authorities were unable to obtain adequate funding and declared bankruptcy in 1880. From 1883 to 1888 it served as an Anglican high school under the name Lincoln College. The building remained empty until 1896 when it was refurbished by the Révérends Frères de la Charité of Montreal for use as a catholic commercial school known as Collège Mont-Saint-Bernard.
(*Dominion Illustrated* [*Montreal*], *18 April 1891, p. 375.*)

44

Collège Notre-Dame
3791 Queen Mary Road, Montreal, Quebec
Constructed: 1880–81
Architects: François and D.A. Lapointe
Material: Stone

Although the architects for the college are identified as François and D.A. Lapointe, they apparently adopted with minor modifications an earlier design presented by prominent Montreal architect H.M. Perrault which was rejected by college officials. The building was intended to provide space for classrooms and student dormitories. True to the eclectic spirit of the age, the design combines Second Empire features with others borrowed from the Gothic Revival style, popular at that time in religious architecture. The original structure, now the central section of the enlarged building, was a plain mansard-roofed block with a central mansarded pavilion. The ecclesiastical affiliations of the college were expressed through the use of pointed gothic openings for the windows and door of the central pavilion and through the slender steeple (never built) that was meant to surmount the earth-bound tower. The added wings on each side of the building are sympathetic to the original design.
(*Canadian Inventory of Historic Building.*)

43

45
Saint Boniface College
Provencher Avenue, Saint Boniface, Manitoba
Constructed: 1879–81 *Destroyed by fire:* 1922
Architect: Balston C. Kenway
Material: Brick

The moving force behind the construction of Saint Boniface College was Monseigneur Alexandre Taché, Archbishop of Saint Boniface, whose determination to educate the French-speaking population of Manitoba is well known. This particular building, situated in a wooded area east of the old college and cathedral, housed the principal Catholic school in Manitoba at that time. Monseigneur Taché perhaps chose Kenway as his architect because of his familiarity with ecclesiastical construction: prior to his arrival in Winnipeg, Kenway had been architect and overseer for extensive renovations to the Old Stone Church in Saint John, New Brunswick. The contractors for Saint Boniface College were Gill and Mould, and J.B. Morache. Clearly functional in design and detail, the college falls naturally into the tradition of mansard-roofed buildings so familiar in ecclesiastical circles in Quebec. Only the central pavilion with its convex-ribbed tower makes an explicit reference to Second Empire sources. Early in the 20th century, wings were added to each side of the original structure.
(*Provincial Archives of Manitoba.*)

46
Sacred Heart Convent, F.C.J.
219 19th Avenue S.W., Calgary, Alberta
Constructed: 1893–94
Additions: 1924
Material: Stone

In 1885 the Sisters, Faithful Companions of Jesus established the first private school in Calgary, offering a full education in both English and French to girls from Roman Catholic families. Several years later, under the direction of the Superior of the Convent, Reverend Mother Mary Greene, this building was erected to provide more space for classrooms and living quarters for the Sisters and boarders. The builder and contractor was Thomas Underwood. Although the design for the Convent lacks the plasticity found in fancy Second Empire buildings, it nevertheless has such features as the mansard roof, central pavilion and a pleasing rhythm of semicircular openings. As it appears in this early photograph, the Sacred Heart Convent corresponds to a description found in the Annals of the Sisters, who were evidently well pleased with the structure. "The exterior of the house is nicely finished off. The pillared portico surrounds the front door, on the top of which is a balcony, to which we have access by a double glass door, opening from the hall of the second storey. Above this balcony in a niche covered with glass stands an exquisite statue of the Sacred Heart, 5-1/2 feet high, the gift of the Rev. Father Lacombe, O.M.I., who pronounces the building a perfect success and a credit both to the workmen and to those who planned the edifice."
(*Public Archives Canada.*)

46

47
Molson Bank
288 Saint James Street West, Montreal, Quebec
Constructed: 1866
Architect: George Browne
Material: Stone

Built in 1866 the Molson Bank represents an early and formative stage of Second Empire in Canada. The self-contained block plan is simpler than the complex pavilion massing of high-style Second Empire and the roof, while gaining in prominence, has not yet taken on its full bombastic dimensions nor acquired the lively silhouette so characteristic of this style by the early 1870s. Nevertheless, the feeling of richness and plasticity created by the broken wall planes and projecting cornices, the baroque quality of the rich garlanded consoles of the attic storey (a motif prominently featured on the New Louvre), and the use of iron cresting and tall chimneys all anticipate the arrival of Second Empire.

George Browne, born in Belfast in 1811, was one of Canada's most prominent and brilliant architects of the 19th century. The Molson Bank was a late work, yet even at this advanced stage in his career he was able to incorporate new stylistic trends. It is not surprising, however, that Browne should have responded so enthusiastically to this new fashion for, as has been pointed out in J. Douglas Stewart's essay on Browne's Kingston architecture, his style always had an element of the "neo-baroque" in its material, texture, mass, and effects of light and shade. These characteristics can be found in the Molson Bank where, under the influence of the Second Empire style, they become enriched and accentuated.

(Canadian Inventory of Historic Building.)

48
Dominion Bank
King Street West at Yonge Street, Toronto, Ontario
Constructed: 1877–79 *Demolished:* Before 1914
Material: Stone
From the year of its founding in 1871 until 1879 the Dominion
Bank was housed in a leased storefront office on King Street
East. The construction of a permanent banking house in 1877–
was seen as a symbol of the Bank's maturity; the lavishness of
the design, heavily ornamented with rich classical detail, would
have offered further assurance to the public of the wealth and
financial stability of this institution. The use of a corner entrance
was a common compositional device for buildings located at
an intersection; the rounded corner created a smooth visual
transition between two façades at right angles to each other.
Although enlarged in 1884, probably by the three-bay section
visible to the left of the photograph, the Dominion Bank had
outgrown this building by the early 20th century and in 1914 wa
replaced by a new head office designed by the Toronto archite
tural firm of Darling and Pearson.
(*Public Archives Canada*.)

49
View of Wellington Street in 1896
Ottawa, Ontario
This photograph of 1896, depicting from left to right, La Banque
Nationale, the Bank of Ottawa and a corner of the Quebec Bank,
illustrates the unified architectural character of Wellington Street
in the post confederation era. Many features, such as the rusticated ground floor, round-headed windows and banded columns were borrowed from the new Post Office of 1873 (Fig. 19)
which marked the eastern end of the street and these motifs were
repeated further west in the design for the Bank of Montreal.
This uniformity was certainly no accident for, following the example set by Baron Haussmann's urban planning in Paris, all building along Wellington Street had to be approved by the federal
government. The result was the creation of a grand Second
Empire thoroughfare which provided Canadians with an imposing symbol of the power and stability of their new nation.
(*Public Archives Canada.*)

50
Eastern Townships Bank
Head Office
241 Dufferin Street, Sherbrooke, Quebec
Constructed: 1875–76
Architect: James Nelson
Material: Stone
Branch Offices:
(1) 191 Principale Street, Richmond, Quebec
Constructed: 1876 *Material:* Brick
(2) 225 Principale Street, Cowansville, Quebec
Constructed: 1874–75 *Material:* Brick
(3) 19 Gerin Lajoie Street, Coaticook, Quebec
Constructed: 1873–74 *Material:* Brick

By the mid-1870s the Eastern Townships Bank founded in 1859 had, according to its annual report of 1873, increased its business to such an extent that many of its old buildings were no longer adequate in size. Between 1873 and 1876 a head office in Sherbrooke and three branch offices in Richmond, Cowansville and Coaticook were constructed, all of which were designed in the Second Empire style. For the branch offices the Directors were "fully aware of the objections in the minds of some of the shareholders to an expenditure on what is called 'bricks and mortar'," and for this reason a very simple, standardized plan, which looks more like a residential building, was adopted, keeping the average cost of construction to $6,000. All three of these buildings have survived but none still functions as a bank.
(*Dominion Illustrated* [*Montreal*], *30 August 1890, p. 133.*)

51
Eastern Townships Bank
241 Dufferin Street, Sherbrooke, Quebec
Constructed: 1875–76
Architect: James Nelson
Material: Stone

A design for the new Head Office in Sherbrooke was not approached with the economical restraint shown for the branch banks. The Annual Report of 1874 states that "the Directors feel also that in a work of this kind ... they are justified in having a handsome as well as useful building, and they believe that the shareholders will agree with them in the opinion that while extravagance should be avoided, yet there is something due to the position of the Bank as one of the most successful institutions in the country."

James Nelson, prominent Montreal architect, was commissioned to prepare the plans and the $37,000 construction contract was awarded to Mr. Quigley and Company, "late of Québec." A new rear wing was added in 1903. This building still functions as a bank, serving as the branch office of the Canadian Imperial Bank of Commerce since its amalgamation in 1911. (*Canadian Inventory of Historic Building.*)

52
The Victoria Block in 1879

53
Victoria Block
15–17 Victoria Street, Clinton, Ontario
Constructed: 1877–78
Builders: William Cooper and Thomas Mackenzie
Material: Brick
Typical of commercial building, the Victoria Block has compressed the sculptural massing of the high Second Empire style into a compact, rectangular plan. The projecting tower and the central focus of the façade create the illusion of the characteristic pavilion plan without its space-wasting projections on the street front. But for the loss of the roof cresting and alterations to the storefront windows the building has changed little over its 100-year history and even today it remains a prominent feature of the town's streetscape.

William Cooper and Thomas Mackenzie owned a planing mill and ran a successful contracting business in Clinton. It has not been determined whether they were responsible for the design of the Victoria Block or whether they were working under the direction of a yet unknown architect.
(*Drawing, H. Belden and Company, Illustrated Historical Atlas of Huron County, Ontario* [*1879; reprint ed., Belleville, Ontario: Mika Silk Screening, 1972*], *p. 18; photograph, Canadian Inventory of Historic Building.*)

52

Victoria Block, Clinton, Ont.

54
Saint James Street, Montreal, Quebec
Looking south along Saint James Street, the four-storey building on the right in the foreground was erected in 1871 for the City and District Savings Bank. Across St. John Street on the other corner is the enormous structure built by Thomas Barron and known as Barron Block (Fig. 55).
(*Public Archives Canada.*)

55
Barron Block
Saint James Street, Montreal, Quebec
Constructed: 1870–72
Architect: Michel Laurent
Material: Stone

This massive commercial block, situated at the corner of Saint James and Saint John streets in what was referred to as "one of the most princely parts of the city," provided prestigious office space for the Montreal business community. While economic considerations may have determined the use of a block plan which made maximum use of the expensive urban lot, its embellishment was certainly not fettered by any sense of frugality. The four-storey design has been punctuated by large, arched windows surrounded by pilasters and finely carved stone decorations. Each floor is divided by a heavy entablature which breaks forward at intervals to be supported by columns of the ornate Corinthian order. Despite the simplicity of the plan this lavish plastic ornamentation gave the building a palatial appearance appropriate for offices of many of the city's merchant princes.

(*Canadian Illustrated News* [*Montreal*], *27 Aug. 1870, p. 136.*)

56
Odell Block
172-184 Wellington Street North, Sherbrooke, Quebec
Constructed: between 1877 and 1881
Material: Brick

Construction of the Odell Block, now known as the Gregoire
Building, was probably begun soon after 1877 when the owner,
Thomas B. Odell, purchased from a Mr. Long a small parcel of
land adjoining his own property on Wellington Street which together made up the site of his new building. The construction
contract was awarded to G.B. Précourt but the design was very
likely the work of an outside, yet unnamed architect. Following
the standard arrangement for a business block the ground floor
was "divided into a number of large and spacious stores... .
The upper flats of the building being occupied by lawyers, notar-
ies and insurance agents." The Odell Block, typical of large
commercial buildings of the Second Empire style, was distinguished, however, in its original form by the extensive use of oval
dormers that lined the mansard roof – since replaced by the
present round- and flat-headed dormers.
(*Canadian Inventory of Historic Building.*)

57

233–237 Dundas Street, London, Ontario

Constructed: 1875

Material: Brick

Commercial blocks such as this could have been found in most urban centres across Canada of the 1870s and 1880s. Unlike the often grand and lavishly executed Second Empire designs constructed for public and even commercial institutions such as banks, these commercial blocks, generally built as investment properties to be leased out, did not function as architectural symbols representing a specific organization. The designs tended to reflect greater economy, in order to provide a maximum return for the investor. The typical solution, as illustrated by the Dundas Street block, was a building compact in plan, making full use of the expensive urban lot but sufficiently rich and grand in detail to attract an affluent clientele.

(*Canadian Inventory of Historic Building*.)

58
Osler Block
5–7 Main Street, Dundas, Ontario
Constructed: Before 1875
Material: Brick

As it appears today Osler Block has been stripped of all its
festive Second Empire dress resulting in its present austere
appearance. In its original condition, iron cresting trimmed the
roof, carved woodwork decorated the dormer windows and
an additional tripartite dormer with semicircular openings accented the small projecting pavilion. Only the coloured and patterned shingles of the mansard roof preserve a hint of its once
picturesque demeanor. The second storey remains unchanged
but the ground floor has been completely altered by the loss of
a plate-glass store-front which occupied the four right-hand bays
and by the removal of the decorative pediments which defined
the windows and two main doorways, one centrally placed on the
façade and the other on the far left-hand side of the building.

Osler Block was built as an investment property for Briton Bath
Osler, a prominent Hamilton lawyer and entrepreneur who re-
sided in Dundas. The ground floor was leased as office space
while the second floor was, and still is, occupied by the local
Masonic Lodge.
(*Canadian Inventory of Historic Building.*)

59

Gerrie Block

Princess Street, Winnipeg, Manitoba

Constructed: 1881 *Demolished:* ca. 1956

Architect: Charles A. Barber

Material: Brick

Gerrie Block is one of a series of warehouses built in this district during the years of Winnipeg's rapid expansion. The six attached brick structures known as Gerrie Block were erected by R. Gerrie and Company for wholesale mercantile purposes. In spite of the utilitarian function of the warehouses, the design is an attractive version of Second Empire, especially in the handling of the mansard roof with its cresting, patterned shingles and semicircular dormers. The potential monotony of the broad roof is relieved through the rhythmic articulation of individual units, punctuated by ribs and carved finials. Although economic considerations are evident in the careful use of the city lot and the modest ornamentation, Gerrie Block is, in the context of warehouse construction, a fashionable and well-appointed building.

(Provincial Archives of Manitoba.)

60

Windsor Hotel

Peel Street, Montreal, Quebec

Constructed: 1876–78 *Demolished:* ca. 1960

Architect: William W. Boyington

Material: Stone

One of the finest examples of Second Empire design in Canada was Montreal's Windsor Hotel. At the time of its erection, it ranked among the most luxurious hostelries in North America. Contemporary observers praised its elegant fittings including "the main dining-hall with its marble floors, gigantic mirrors, and lovely landscape paintings," the grand promenade which "fairly bewilders the eye with its splendour," the bridal chamber, a "charming *bijou*" with velvet carpet and furniture in silk, and the entrance hall which "reminds the traveller of some of those grand old Italian palaces." To complete this vast project at the cost of almost one million dollars, the sponsors engaged an American architect experienced in hotel construction, William W. Boyington of Chicago, and drew on numerous local and American firms and craftsmen. The first lessee was J.W. Worthington of Montreal. The impact made by the Windsor Hotel is well summed up by a contemporary traveller from Britain who writes that "the rooms of the Windsor at Montreal fairly astonished us. There is nothing in the hotel way in London comparable to the house, except perhaps the Grand at Charring Cross and if adjectives must be used I could say the Windsor was the grander of the two."

(Public Archives Canada.)

61
Long's Hotel (now Prince of Wales Hotel)
6 Picton Street, Niagara-on-the-Lake, Ontario
Constructed: 1883–85
Material: Brick
By the 1870s Niagara-on-the-Lake had lost its position as a prominent commercial and political centre and had assumed its present role as a tranquil resort town. With the arrival of the tourist many new hotels had to be built in the 1870s and 1880s and of course most were designed in the popular Second Empire fashion. Long's Hotel, later known as Niagara House, the Arlington Hotel and finally as the Prince of Wales Hotel, was built for William Long. According to a late-19th-century tourist brochure it "enjoyed a well earned reputation for first class service, at moderate prices ... Large airy rooms and the best of board can be obtained here for $7 a week and upwards." A modest but respectable resort hotel, it could be described as ranking midway between the Windsor Hotel in Montreal (Fig. 60) and the Yale Hotel in Vancouver (Fig. 62) on the quality scale for hotel accommodation.
(*Prince of Wales Hotel, Niagara-on-the-Lake*.)

62

Colonial Hotel (now Yale Hotel)

1300 Granville Street, Vancouver, British Columbia

Constructed: 1888–89

Material: Brick

The Colonial Hotel, known as the Yale Hotel since 1907, would never have had a reputation as one of Vancouver's fashionable inns. Situated in the industrialized False Creek area in the working class neighbourhood of Yaletown, chiefly populated by Canadian Pacific Railway employees from the nearby train yard, it provided low-priced accommodation and became well known as the centre of the notorious Yaletown nightlife.

This plain blockish design punctuated by round-headed windows was poor cousin to the posh, palatial Second Empire hotel like the Windsor Hotel in Montreal (Fig. 60); yet the survival of the mansard roof indicates a direct stylistic descendency. Undistinguished mansarded hotels like the Yale could have been found with remarkable consistency in any number of cities and towns across the country until the end of the 19th century. The mansard roof became so closely associated with hotel accommodation that this form survived well beyond the heyday of the Second Empire style.

(*Canadian Inventory of Historic Building*.)

63

North Street Terminal, Intercolonial Railway
North Street, Halifax, Nova Scotia
Constructed: 1874–77 *Destroyed:* 1917
Architect: Railway Department, Department of Public Works
Material: Brick

Contrary to the general policy of the Intercolonial Railway to build economically, the North Street terminal featured the expensive Second Empire style. Because the railway station provided the visitor with his first impression of a city, it was felt that a major urban centre such as Halifax required a building appropriate to its status. This symbolic role was observed in an 1897 publication: "Supposing one is to arrive in the city by train, he is at once impressed with the idea that he has reached an important terminal point, for he finds himself in one of the finest depots ... east of Boston."

Prominent local builder Henry Peters received the contract to build the main body of the station. The mansard roof was prefabricated in Philadelphia by Clarke, Reeves and Company, one of several American firms which mass-produced cast-iron architectural elements. The North Street terminal was destroyed in the Halifax explosion of 1917.

(W.H. Howard, Halifax of Today: An Illustrated Souvenir of the Queen's Diamond Jubilee, 1837–97 [Halifax: W.H. Howard, 1897], n.p.)

64
William Bell Organ Factory
Carden Street, Guelph, Ontario
Constructed: 1881
Material: Yellow brick
Suited to its utilitarian function, the façade of the William Bell
Organ Factory has reduced the grid system of the Second Empire style to a series of simple horizontal and vertical bands
applied to a flat, unbroken wall plane. Above the cornice, however, this undistinguished block has been dressed up – patterned shingles, iron cresting, flagpoles, and corner clock tower
– giving it an air of picturesque gaiety which disguises the
functional design below.

The William Bell Organ Company, later to become the Bell
Organ Company, was in business from 1865 to 1930 and was
said to have been the largest reed organ company in the British
Empire with branch offices in London, England and South Africa.
Although some of the original walls of the Guelph factory are
still standing much of the building was destroyed in a fire of 1940
and in another of 1975.
(*Historical Atlas Publishing Co., Historical Atlas of Wellington
County* [*reprint ed. of 1906, Wellington County: Corporation of
the County of Wellington, 1972*], *p. 14.*)

65
Chinic Warehouse
47 Dalhousie Street, Quebec, Quebec
Constructed: 1871
Architect: Joseph-Ferdinand Peachy
Material: Brick
Seven years before the opening of Dalhousie Street, the group of
shops standing on this site was demolished to make way for
this large warehouse. As originally constructed, the buff firebrick
building had an eight-bay façade surmounted by a mansard
roof. A firewall projected above the roofline and divided the
building into two separate sections. The overall massing of elements had considerable solidity in contrast to the delicate stone
trim. About 1923, the two western bays were raised three storeys
and at a later date two of the doorways were enlarged. Unfortunately these alterations have undermined the unity of the design.

The Chinic Warehouse was designed by J.F. Peachy, the
Quebec architect who specialized in mansard roofs, and built by
master joiner Isaac Dorion and master mason Pierre Château-
vert. The building was erected by the Compagnie Richelieu
which immediately leased one section to dry goods merchant
George Alford and the other section to Chinic and Beaudet, one
of the oldest hardware companies in the country which began
business under the name F.X. Methot.
(*Canadian Inventory of Historic Building*.)

66

Design for a Villa, Mount Royal, Montreal, Quebec

Published: 1875

Architect: Gilbert Bostwick Croff

The architectural pattern book played an essential role in the rapid dissemination of the Second Empire style across the United States and Canada. Some of the most popular and influential of these publications were authored by the American architect, Gilbert Bostwick Croff of Saratoga Springs, New York. Although Croff would have been well known in New York state for a number of mansarded designs for public, commercial and residential building, it was his three publications entitled *Model Suburban Architecture* of 1870, *Original Designs for Entrance Doors* of 1871 and *Progressive American Architecture* of 1875 that earned him widespread renown.

Although these books featured a wide range of styles the dominant thrust was Second Empire. This illustration of "a stately and imposing Villa" in Montreal was typical of Croff's extremely ornate and flamboyant style which strove for, as Croff himself describes, "that picturesque variety of skyline, depth of shadow, and sweet repose so charming in an architectural conception."

In Canada, Croff's work was known in Montreal and in Saint John, New Brunswick, where he opened a successful branch office in 1877 (Fig. 84); however, the indirect influence of his pattern books on other architects and builders was probably much more widespread. Although it is impossible to determine the extent of this influence without further study, suburban villas such as those illustrated in Belleville, Ontario (Figs. 71, 72) and in Madoc (Fig. 68) bear a strong resemblance to the Croff style. (*Gilbert Bostwick Croff, Progressive American Architecture* [*New York: Orange Judd and Company (1875)*], *Pl. 40.*)

67

405 Broad Street West, Dunnville, Ontario

Constructed: 1889

Material: Brick

Although constructed in 1889 at a time when the popularity of the Second Empire style was declining, the design of this suburban residence, with its symmetrical plan accented by a central projecting frontispiece and the convex mansard roof enlivened by a broken silhouette, patterned shingles and iron cresting, reveals little change in Second Empire domestic architecture as it had developed in Ontario nearly 20 years earlier. It was built for dry goods merchant Donald McDonald and, with the exception of a rear addition of 1940 designed by Frances Brown, the building has been altered little over the years.

(*Canadian Inventory of Historic Building*.)

68

John C. Dale House
195 Elgin Street, Madoc, Ontario
Material: Brick

Like so many grand Second Empire mansions the palatial character of the Dale House has been greatly enhanced by its imposing site on top of a hill and its twelve acres of landscaped garden, complete with orchards, a walkway through pine trees, and a bridal path. According to local research the Dale House was built for the owner of a local private bank, John C. Dale, between 1904 and 1910. However, a stylistic comparison with two other Second Empire residences in the area, namely Glanmore (Fig. 71) and 201 Charles Street (Fig. 72) both located in nearby Belleville, would suggest an earlier date for this building. Many similarities – the massing, the arrangement of bay windows and verandahs, the grouping and proportions of the dormer window, the curved profile of the mansard roof, and the decorative detail of the cornice, window surrounds and doorway – lead one to suspect that the Dale House dates from the 1880s, contemporary with the Belleville examples. It may even be the work of the same architect, Thomas Hanley.

(*Canadian Inventory of Historic Building.*)

69
Lorne Hall
3 Meredith Crescent, Toronto, Ontario
Constructed: 1876
Material: Brick

This grand suburban villa was one of the early homes to be erected in the fashionable Rosedale area. Its first resident was prominent Toronto businessman, William Davies, who founded a meat-packing business which was to become Canada Packers in 1927. It was christened Lorne Hall by William Perkins Bull who resided here from 1906 to 1943.

The design of this house can be compared in many respects to the design for Government House (Fig. 14) by Henry Langley. Although Lorne Hall is on a more modest scale, both are characterized by a symmetrical composition with a centrally placed tower. An even closer parallel can be established in a comparison between the design and location of the porches. Both display porches on the main entrance and a longer verandah at the side; both are surmounted by balustrades and articulated by the unusual arch motif with rounded corners joined by a slightly raised lintel. These similarities might be the result of an attempt to imitate the prestigious Government House or perhaps an indication of a common architect.

(*Canadian Inventory of Historic Building*.)

70

Fontbonne Hall

534 Queens Avenue, London, Ontario

Constructed: 1878

Material: Brick

Queens Avenue was London's residential showplace of the 1870s and Fontbonne Hall was one of its finest architectural achievements. Built for William Spencer, president of the newly amalgamated London Oil and Refining Company, it is an impressive monument to the new wealth generated by the oil discovery at Petrolia in 1861. The design maintains the symmetrical composition characteristic of public building, but the detailing, with its ornate bracketed cornice and large two-storey bay windows accented by slender stone columns, has been handled with a lighter and more festive touch. The treatment of the roof, distinctive for its lively play of planes and curved shapes, adds an attractive finishing touch. The porch and large brick wing are recent additions.

(*Canadian Inventory of Historic Building*.)

71
Architectural Drawing for Glanmore
257 Bridge Street, Belleville, Ontario
Constructed: 1882–83
Architect: Thomas Hanley
Material: Brick
The Second Empire style, when applied to domestic architecture, often takes on a more refined and elegant air than the robust massing and forms characteristic of public building. Glanmore, originally built for wealthy banker and financier, John Philpot Curran Phillips, and now housing the Hastings County Museum, offers one of Ontario's most elaborate examples of this taste. Features such as the asymmetrical massing, the gentle concave curve of the roof, the delicate woodwork of the dormer windows, and the bracketed cornice with scalloped frieze accenting the pattern of window openings below, create an appearance of picturesque elegance – a quality strongly advocated for domestic building in American architectural pattern books.

The designer, Thomas Hanley, is listed in the Belleville directories as a carpenter, builder and architect from 1878 to 1902. Nothing is yet known of his origins or training; however, judging from his design for Glanmore he was either an architect of considerable skill or a very clever copyist of comtemporary pattern books.
(*Hastings County Museum*.)

72
201 Charles Street, Belleville, Ontario

Constructed: ca. 1879
Material: Brick

Belleville was well endowed with a number of fine Second Empire houses, probably the legacy of local architect/builder Thomas Hanley. Although Glanmore (Fig. 71) is the only documented example of his work, 201 Charles Street, built for local physican Dr. Potts and first listed in the Belleville city directories in 1879–80, bears all the outward signs of a Hanley design. Similar in plan, roof shape, arrangement of window openings and verandahs, and almost identical in the minute detail of the porches, in the fretted ornaments above the dormers, and in the decoration of the upper or deck cornice, 201 Charles Street provides an attractive companion piece to Glanmore and confirms Hanley's position as an important designer of Second Empire domestic architecture.

(*Canadian Inventory of Historic Building*.)

73
William G. Perley House
415 Wellington Street, Ottawa, Ontario
Constructed: ca. 1875 *Demolished*
Material: Brick
The Second Empire style which dominated the Wellington streetscape was not restricted to public and commercial building. The Perley House, situated on the present site of the National Library and Public Archives Building, provided a residential complement to the dignified parade of mansarded government buildings and banks which lined Wellington Street. Built around 1875 for William G. Perley, co-owner of the Ottawa lumber company, Perley and Pattee, and later a member of Parliament, this immense brick residence showed a refinement and sophistication on such features as the porches, bay window and dormers that was unusual for domestic buildings in Ottawa but appropriate to its location on the most prestigious street in the new nation's capital.
(*Public Archives Canada.*)

74
Wyoming
67 Queen Street, Guelph, Ontario
Constructed: 1866–67 *Enlarged:* ca. 1880
Material: Stone
Instead of building anew many owners of older houses gave their residences a Second Empire up-date by adding a mansard roof. As originally built in 1866–67 for wealthy dry goods merchant, John Hogg, 67 Queen Street was a small one-storey building constructed of the characteristic Guelph limestone and idyllically situated on the crest of a hill on Queen Street in a five-acre park-like setting. In 1880 Hogg sold the entire property to James W. Lyon, owner of the internationally known World Publishing Company and Guelph's first millionaire. By adding an extra storey, a mansard roof, and servants' quarters at the rear, Lyon transformed this small cottage into a palatial Second Empire mansion which he renamed Wyoming.
(*Canadian Inventory of Historic Building*.)

75
Hallowell Township, Prince Edward County, Ontario
Material: Brick
This farmhouse in Hallowell Township provides a notable exception to the generalization that Second Empire is predominantly an urban and suburban style. Its picturesque effect comes from the asymmetrical composition with off-centre tower and the wealth of iron cresting and carved ornamentation. The characteristic round dormer windows and intricate cornice brackets on this elegant residence demonstrate a sophisticated awareness of Second Empire design that is unusual in a rural area.
(*Canadian Inventory of Historic Building*.)

75

76

125 Rosemount Avenue, Weston, Ontario

Material: Brick

Today, the town of Weston has been consumed by Metropolitan Toronto as part of the Borough of York, but houses such as 125 Rosemount Avenue provide glimpses of the original character of the town when it was a small, independent manufacturing centre to the northwest of Toronto. While it is often a tendency in smaller residential buildings to reduce the Second Empire style to the use of a mansard roof, 125 Rosemount Avenue, despite its modest scale, reflects a sophisticated use of Second Empire forms. The asymmetrical massing, the picturesque play of receding wall and roof planes, and ornate dormers and verandahs recall grand Second Empire mansions found throughout Ontario.

(*Canadian Inventory of Historic Building*.)

77

29 West Street, Brantford, Ontario

Constructed: Post 1875

Material: Brick

This one-and-a-half storey, symmetrical design is a continuation of a traditional building type often referred to as the "Ontario cottage"; but in this case, there has been a Second Empire update with the addition of a mansard roof and bay windows. It is obviously the work of a local builder as is indicated by the unsophisticated handling of the top-heavy mansard roof and the rather stiff interpretation of the characteristic round dormer window. The lively colour scheme of patterned shingles captures a delightful sense of the picturesque.

(*Canadian Inventory of Historic Building*.)

77

78
332–344 Rubidge Street, Peterborough, Ontario
Constructed: 1884–85
Material: Brick

This residential row in Peterborough represents the height of Second Empire fashion in terrace housing. By uniting the individual units into one compositional scheme of balanced projecting pavilions, the architect has avoided the monotonous repetition of identical units that so often characterizes row housing and has captured that sense of monumentality reminiscent of grand public building in the Second Empire vein.

It was built for George Cox, a wealthy insurance baron and entrepreneur from Peterborough as an investment property. Although the architect has not yet been documented, its design is identical to another terrace block in Winnipeg constructed in 1882 by the firm of architects, Wilmot and Stewart, a fact which suggests the use of these same architects or at least the same plans.

(*Canadian Inventory of Historic Building*.)

79

119–133 Spruce Street, Toronto, Ontario

Constructed: 1887

Material: Brick

Although by 1887 the Second Empire style was well past the height of fashion, the mansard roof did not entirely disappear from use. Its appeal was both practical and aesthetic for as seen in this modest terrace unit in Toronto the mansard roof provided two full storeys but with an added touch of the picturesque in its steep front slope decorated with dormer windows, patterned shingles, and iron cresting. By this device, the builder avoided the monotonous form of the alternative two-storey box with a flat roof.

(*Canadian Inventory of Historic Building*.)

80

322 Dundas Street East, Toronto, Ontario
Constructed: 1886–87
Material: Brick
This house forms one of a series of almost identical buildings on
the north side of Dundas Street. It is located on the fringes of
the once fashionable Sherbourne Street and, despite the narrowness of the lot, the insistence on a single detached unit instead
of a less expensive row house indicates an attempt to maintain a
prestigious look to the neighbourhood. The heavy bracketed
cornice and fancy dormers capture some of the richness of the
Second Empire style but the narrowness of the façade and the
height of each storey produce an elongated and pinched
appearance.
(*Canadian Inventory of Historic Building.*)

81
Farmhouse
Maitland, Hants County, Nova Scotia
Material: Wood
This small farmhouse represents a blending of the Second Empire style with a well-established Maritime building tradition. The
mansard roof and the taste for richer surface ornamentation
are drawn from Second Empire design; however, these elements
only thinly disguise the familiar compact, squarely proportioned
building with symmetrical façade decorated with doric pilasters
and segmental pediments and shelves, characteristic of an older
Maritime building type in the classical vernacular tradition. The
projecting frontispiece imitates the pavilion massing of the Second Empire style but, again, this form, minus the mansard roof,
was already well entrenched in the Maritime building vocabulary.
(*Canadian Inventory of Historic Building*.)

82
Quinniapiac
25 Winter Avenue, Saint John's, Newfoundland
Constructed: ca. 1885
Material: Wood
Quinniapiac imparts a distinctly Maritime flavour to the Second
Empire style due to its use of clapboard and its rich application of
intricately carved wood ornamentation. The large triple-paned
dormer motif is a characteristic feature of the Maritimes. When
the dormers are seen in conjunction with the bay windows on the
ground floor an effect similar to the projecting pavilions of high-
style Second Empire is created. As originally built for Prescott
Emerson, a judge of the Newfoundland Supreme Court, Quinniapiac had a tower and conservatory; however, both were removed
in the early years of the 20th century.
(*Canadian Inventory of Historic Building*.)

83

49 Rennies Mill Road, Saint John's, Newfoundland
Constructed: 1885
Material: Brick

This building was welcomed with enthusiastic praise by the Sai
John's *Evening Telegram* on March 23, 1885, which described
it as "the magnificent residence which has just been erected
by Mr. (Alexander) Marshall in that fasionable suburb locality
known as Rennies Mill Road. It stands as a monument of succe
in business, an ornament to the neighbourhood and a most con
vincing proof of the mechanical skill and ingenuity of our native
workmen." This fine residence would have been particularly
outstanding since it was built of "Boston" and "Bangor" brick
instead of the usual wood; yet, despite the use of these atypical
materials, a distinct Maritime appearance has been retained. T
delicate and whimsical treatment of the stonework and the colo
ful panels of white enamelled brick under the eaves recall the
intricacy and fluidity of detail common to Maritime building in
wood.

This same article identified John Score, a local man, as the
builder. No mention of an architect was made; however, althouc
it was not unusual for builders to provide their own designs, the
sophistication of this building would suggest the work of a yet
unknown architect.
(*Canadian Inventory of Historic Building.*)

84

99 Wentworth Street, Saint John, New Brunswick
Constructed: 1877–78
Architects: Gilbert Bostwick Croff and F.T. Camp
Material: Brick

The firm of Croff and Camp from Saratoga Springs, New York, opened a Saint John office in 1877, probably in order to capitalize on the building boom created by the great fire earlier that year. Croff was already well known for his numerous public and private commissions primarily in the state of New York and for several publications of his architectural designs (Fig. 66). With these credentials, his firm was quickly accepted by the Saint John community.

The house on Wentworth Street, built for local druggist A. Chipman Smith, is one of the many buildings designed by this firm in Saint John. A contemporary report on the construction in the *Daily Telegraph* describes this "Handsome French Cottage" as having "a graceful, well-proportioned tower that will rise to an elevation of seventeen feet above the cresting line of the mansard roof, with flowing frieze and angular pediments which will, with the bold chimney tops, give the entire structure a most graceful and pleasing outline." The building was also praised for its modern conveniences in heating and plumbing, providing "an interesting and suggestive model in both beauty and convenience."
(*Canadian Inventory of Historic Building*.)

85

354 Main Street, Saint John, New Brunswick
Constructed: 1875
Material: Brick

Perched high on a hill commanding a spectacular view over Saint John, this palatial mansion certainly merits its name, "the Castle." Although the use of brick, the large scale, and the asymmetrical massing with corner tower are more akin to Second Empire residential building in Ontario, the characteristic Maritime taste for abundant surface detail is clearly evident. In fact, this quality as seen in features such as the elaborate cornice molding with finely carved scroll brackets and panelled frieze fringed with fretted ornaments, the delicately incised window surrounds capped with the broken curve of the entablature, and the lightly carved detail of the veranda, has rarely been expressed in such an exuberant and lavish manner.

"The Castle" was built about 1875 for Count Robert Visart De Bury of Belgium who, having married into the well-known Simonds family of Saint John, moved to Portland (now a part of Saint John) in 1873 where he served for many years as Belgian Consul to New Brunswick and Consular Agent for France at Saint John and was, for a number of years, a member of the Portland Town Council.

(*Canadian Inventory of Historic Building*.)

86

High Street, Souris East, Prince Edward Island
Constructed: Before 1880
Material: Wood

A common design characteristic of small domestic building in the Second Empire style which appears most frequently in the Maritimes is the tendency of the mansard roof to dominate the overall design. The house at Souris East, built for Dr. P.A. McIntyre, Lieutenant-Governor of Prince Edward Island from 1899 to 1904, offers a good example of this tendency. The unusually steep upper roof slopes produce a very high mansard roof that overpowers the supporting walls.

(*Canadian Inventory of Historic Building*.)

87

1173 South Park Street, Halifax, Nova Scotia
Constructed: Between 1888 and 1895
Material: Wood
At the end of the 19th century the recovery of the Halifax economy after two decades of stagnation encouraged a rapid growth in the city's population. The house at 1173 South Park Street is a typical product of the extensive suburban development intended to meet the housing needs of the expanding community. Despite the waning popularity of the Second Empire style at this time, the use of the mansard roof and the regional feature of the bay dormer over the bay window indicate the persistent hold of this style on building in the Atlantic provinces.
(*Canadian Inventory of Historic Building*.)

88
37 Mecklenburg Street, Saint John, New Brunswick
Constructed: between 1877 and 1882
Material: Wood
The great fire of 1877 devastated much of Saint John at the
height of the Second Empire craze. As a result, much of the
consequent rebuilding reflected this current architectural fashion. Although many chose to rebuild in more fire-resistant brick,
the house at 37 Mecklenburg, constructed for the Eaton family to
replace the home they had lost in the fire, was fairly typical of
residential building in the post-fire period. This one-and-a-half
storey building with double bay windows capped by triple-paned
bay dormers repeats a familiar Maritime type. The use of the
oval dormers, a feature usually associated with large public
buildings, adds a distinctive touch.
(*Canadian Inventory of Historic Building*.)

89
767 Brunswick Street, Fredericton, New Brunswick
Constructed: Post 1882
Material: Wood

Lined with gracious Victorian homes set amid tall elm trees, the Brunswick streetscape captures the dignified atmosphere of a 19th-century residential avenue. The house at 767 Brunswick Street provides one of its finest architectural features. The use of a narrower two-bay façade as opposed to a symmetrical three-bay façade is more characteristic of urban building where the narrower city lot requires a more compact plan. As a result the design has a much stronger vertical emphasis which is accentuated by the tall mansard roof and by the upward thrust of the typical Maritime feature, the double bay window with a triple-paned bay dormer. An accurate date of construction has not yet been determined but the house was probably built soon after the purchase of the lot by Alexander Sterling in 1882.
(*Canadian Inventory of Historic Building*.)

90
A.R. Dickey House
169 Victoria Street East, Amherst, Nova Scotia
Material: Wood
Arthur Rupert Dickey (1857–1900), the son of R.B. Dickey, a
father of Confederation, was a noted Nova Scotian lawyer, a
member of Parliament for Cumberland County from 1888 to
1896, and a cabinet minister from 1894 to 1896. His residence in
Amherst is of modest size but handsomely executed in the suita-
bly fashionable Second Empire style. The dormer design with
sides that cut through the eaves line of the roof is a feature
frequently found in the Maritimes.
(*Canadian Inventory of Historic Building*.)

91
917 Loch Lomond Road, Saint John, New Brunswick
Material: Wood
This charming residence, now situated in the outskirts of Saint
John, may be modest in size but is certainly not modest in dress.
Rarely have the decorative possibilities of wood been handled
with such variety and exuberance. The brightly painted carved
details which have been liberally sprinkled over the building and
the contrasting patterns of the wood shingles and horizontal
and diagonal planking produce an exceptionally fanciful version
of the Second Empire style. Typical of the Maritimes are the
dormer windows which cut through the eaves line and are edged
by giant consoles.
(*Canadian Inventory of Historic Building*.)

92
Birchwood
35 Longworth Avenue, Charlottetown, Prince Edward Island
Constructed: 1876
Material: Wood

According to the Charlottetown *Examiner* of June 2, 1877 the
plans for Birchwood were drawn up by the owner, Lemuel Cambridge Owen, an important shipowner and merchant in the community. His house shows an awareness of Second Empire design
in such features as the mansard roof, projecting central pavilion
with its mansarded tower and delicate iron cresting that enlivens
both the verandah and the roof. Yet beneath these elements,
one recognizes the compact form and broader proportions of the
earlier classicizing tradition. This conservative approach would
seem to confirm the hypothesis that an amateur architect was
responsible for the design.
(*Canadian Inventory of Historic Building.*)

93

Queen Hotel

494 Saint George Street, Annapolis Royal, Nova Scotia

Material: Wood

Originally built as a private residence for Thomas Ritchie, the building served as a posh boarding house until 1897 when it became a boys' private school. In 1921 W.C. MacPherson bought the Ritchie House to replace the original Queen Hotel which had burnt down that year. Today it is still known as the Queen Hotel although it now operates as a boarding home for aged.

An unusually grand and showy residence for a small community such as Annapolis Royal, the design reflects that characteristic Maritime taste for minute, intricately carved wood detail in the shaped window surrounds, cornice brackets, and delicate fretted ornaments under the eaves. The addition of an extra cornice molding at the point where the mansard roof changes from concave to convex curve gives the roofline a highly individualistic appearance.

(*Canadian Inventory of Historic Building*.)

94
Ship Cove Road
Burin, Burin Peninsula, Newfoundland
Material: Wood
This modest house would seem to have little in common with the
sumptuous and richly ornamented Second Empire style; yet
the use of the mansard roof links it with the more formal tradition.
Typical of Newfoundland vernacular interpretation are certain
forms like the almost flat upper portion of the mansard and the
dormers which have semicircular windows set into a gable
shape. The projecting central section with flattened tower may
perhaps be a distant echo of the Second Empire pavilion.
(*Canadian Inventory of Historic Building.*)

95
176–182 Gower Street, Saint John's, Newfoundland
Constructed: post 1892
Material: Wood
This type of row house, characterized by clapboard siding and
mansard roof with almost flat upper slopes, was built time and
again after the fire of 1892 which destroyed almost all of the
downtown core of Saint John's. Buildings of this nature can be
found throughout the city and form an essential part of its distinctive architectural character. This plain, economical design is far
removed from the flamboyant and extravagant Second Empire
style; however, the survival of the mansard roof indicates the
lasting mark left by this tradition.
(*Canadian Inventory of Historic Building.*)

95

96

30 Monkstown Road, Saint John's, Newfoundland
Constructed: 1875
Architects: J. and J.T. Southcott
Material: Wood

This residential building is one of a pair of identical structures situated side by side on the fashionable suburban street of Monkstown Road. Both were designed by the father and son team of J. and J.T. Southcott whose names became so closely associated with the Second Empire style in Saint John's that it has been locally referred to as the "Southcott style". The Monkstown Road pair are typical of the Southcotts' Second Empire residences in the use of the bellcast mansard roof, round-headed dormers, and two bay windows on the front. The absence of a prominent front entrance, a product of an interior plan with the central hallway running parallel to the main façade, is an unusual but often repeated feature of Southcott houses. (*Canadian Inventory of Historic Building*.)

97
31 Lincoln Street, Lunenburg, Nova Scotia
Material: Wood
In Lunenburg the mansard roof made a considerable impact although the Second Empire style was modified by established building traditions, imparting a distinctive local flavour to this style. The house at 31 Lincoln Street, constructed of wood, symmetrical in plan and restrained in detail is a typical example of larger domestic building of this style in Lunenburg. The three-sectioned projecting frontispiece, characterized by strong horizontal divisions, is unified by the semicircular forms of the doorway and windows.
(*Engineering and Architecture Branch, Department of Indian and Northern Affairs.*)

98
143 Queen Street, Truro, Nova Scotia
Material: Wood
As seen in an old photograph published in a late 19th-century
pictorial guide to Truro, Queen Street was lined with spacious
Victorian homes situated on ample, well-treed lots – a typical
suburban environment of the late 19th century. These residences
offered a wide range of styles of which the Second Empire style,
as typified by 143 Queen Street, was among the most popular.
By Maritime standards the decoration of 143 Queen Street is
quite reserved, being restricted to light scroll brackets under the
eaves and boxed bay windows, a recurring feature of Second
Empire residences in Truro which contributes to the angular
appearance of the façade.
(*Canadian Inventory of Historic Building*.)

99
Shaughnessy House

1923 Dorchester Street West, Montreal, Quebec
Constructed: 1874–76
Architect: William T. Thomas
Material: Stone

Among the largest of Montreal's stately mansions, the Shaughnessy House was originally a double dwelling built jointly for textile manufacturer Robert Brown and Canadian Pacific Railway magnate Duncan McIntyre. It bears all the standard features of high-style Second Empire including pavilion massing, bay windows, semicircular window openings, and an ornate mansard roof with oval dormers and rich iron cresting. True to Second Empire ideals, it enjoys a wide vista and a pleasing view over the Saint Lawrence River valley. The use of stone, however, puts the stamp of Quebec on this house. The design comes from William T. Thomas, one of Montreal's most prolific architects who specialized in fashionable residences in the Italian manner.
The builders were master builder and mason Charles Lamontagne, and master carpenter and joiner Edward Maxwell. The house has remarkable associations with railway history, having been occupied by such notables as William Van Horne, who lived here from 1882 (the year he became general manager of the Canadian Pacific Railway) until 1891, and Lord Shaughnessy, who moved into the eastern half in 1892 and later took over the entire house when he became president of the Canadian Pacific Railway in 1899.
(*Canadian Inventory of Historic Building*.)

100
3532–3538 Sainte-Famille Street, Montreal, Quebec
Constructed: 1872 (no. 3532); 1876 (no. 3538)
Material: Stone
Built in the 1870s by mercantile agent Charles Gagnon, these two houses reflect the particularities of small-scale development at this period. Gagnon began by occupying the earlier house, and moved four years later to the second house when it was completed. Although most of Sainte-Famille Street was developed at this time, land was owned in small parcels; consequently, houses are generally similar, but specific details are different. Gagnon's pair are typical of Montreal row houses in the Second Empire vein with their façades articulated by projecting pavilions capped by mansarded towers, their high basements serving as full living storeys, and especially in their use of contrasting textures of stone. Although no architect has been identified for the design of Gagnon's houses, it is interesting to note that his next door neighbour was architect A.G. Fowler in 1873 and then architect A.F. Dunlop from 1874–76.
(*Canadian Inventory of Historic Building*.)

101

661–675 Grande Allée East, Quebec, Quebec
Constructed: 1882–83
Architect: Joseph-Ferdinand Peachy
Material: Stone

This residential row on Quebec's most prestigious thoroughfare was put up by Abraham Joseph, a prosperous merchant who occupied a splendid residence on an adjoining site. The specifi- cations called for work of the best quality, including such requir- ments as fine bush-hammered Deschambault stone, without veins, marks or other defects, for the ground storey, and metal- covered roofs similar to the new construction at the Séminaire de Québec (*see* text 42). Following the plans of Joseph-Ferdinand Peachy, the architect who so favoured the Second Empire style, the builders achieved a picturesque effect, by conservative Quebec City standards, through the rugged masonry, bay win- dows, decorative dormers and a mutlitude of brackets. Attractive details like the segmental openings and the door and window surrounds lend coherence to the overall design. The contractors were John O'Leary for masonry, Joseph Garneau for carpentry and joinery, William McDonald for painting and Zepherin Vaudry for plumbing and metalwork. When these houses were com- pleted, two of his sons, Andrew and Montefiore Joseph, active partners in the business, occupied Nos. 665 and 675, residing there until well into the 20th century.
(*Canadian Inventory of Historic Building.*)

102
3837–3893 de Bullion Street, Montreal, Quebec
Constructed: 1876–81
Material: Brick

This long terrace, put up on what used to be called Cadieux Street, occupied most of the city block between Napoleon and Roy streets. Development began in 1876 and houses were gradually added until 1881 when the terrace contained eighteen identical structures. Unlike some of the grand stone terraces in Montreal, this row was built on an economic scale, only one storey in height with inexpensive brick. Token reference to Second Empire influence is given in the slight wall projection on each unit that suggests pavilion massing, the shallow mansard-roofed towers with some iron cresting still intact, and the semicircular dormers. The terrace was intended to provide housing for modest income groups as a random sample of the 1881 street directory confirms. The occupants at that time included merchants, clerks, stenographers, bookkeepers, insurance agents and grocers.
(*Canadian Inventory of Historic Building*.)

103
28 Guénette Street, Lévis, Quebec
Constructed: Before 1889
Material: Brick

This imposing dwelling is just one of several substantialmansa
roofed residences recorded by the Canadian Inventory of Historic Building in Lévis, a concentration that reflects the growth
size and stature of this urban centre in the last quarter of the
19th century. Little is known about the house except that buildi
contractor Joseph Paquet lived here from at least 1889 until
after 1915. Whether Paquet was the original owner and/or buil
is unknown. While the walls are handled in a relatively simple
manner, enlivened mainly by the use of different colours of bric
(a favorite device of Gothic Revival designers), the mansard
roof ranks among the sophisticated characteristics of Second
Empire influence. The curved ribs of the main roof are echoed
the tower, which also features delicate round windows similar t
models illustrated in American pattern books.
(*Canadian Inventory of Historic Building.*)

104
118 Fraser Street, Rivière-du-Loup, Quebec
Constructed: ca. 1880
Material: Brick
This attractive suburban villa in the community of Rivière-du-Loup, formerly known as Fraserville, proves that Second Empire influence extended far beyond Canada's principal cities. Though the wall surfaces are flat and the ornamentation timid, the overall design is appealing for its play of semicircular and segmental forms. A fine touch is the graceful flare of the ribs on the main roof and tower.
(*Canadian Inventory of Historic Building*.)

105
52 Vachon Boulevard, Sainte-Marie-de-Beauce, Quebec
Constructed: 1885
Material: Wood
Shortly after it blossomed in major urban centres, Second Empire
reached the more remote communities in Canada like the
Beauce region south of Quebec City. This residence at Sainte-
Marie-de-Beauce reflects a regional preference for frame and
clapboard construction, but in design, follows the new Second
Empire craze. The sophistication of certain details – the convex
ribbing on the mansarded tower and the round decorative win-
dows – suggests the influence of pattern books from the nearby
northern United States. The architect has not yet been identified.
The house was built for a local merchant, Gédéon Beaucher *dit*
Morency, who sold both house and contents two years later to
notary Georges Théberge when he left Saint-Marie-de-Beauce
for Montreal.
(*Canadian Inventory of Historic Building*.)

106
7214 Royale Avenue, Château Richer, Quebec
Constructed: ca. 1880
Material: Wood
In its main form, this house represents the culmination of the vernacular tradition in rural Quebec, the result of slow evolution over two centuries. Typical features include the one-and-a-half storey height, raised basement, full-length verandah, symmetrical design of the façade and classicizing doorway trim. What is new is the mansard roof. Permitting full use of the attic storey, was probably adopted for its practical advantage rather than for any connection with fashionable Second Empire style. Characteristic of the Quebec interpretation of the two-sided mansard are the marked rise in the upper slope and the bellcast eaves or *larmier* which has such a pronounced extension that it provides shelter for the verandah.
(*Canadian Inventory of Historic Building*.)

107
2 Saint-Joseph Boulevard, Charlesbourg, Quebec
Constructed: ca. 1885
Material: Wood

If one disregards the mansard roof, this building represents the fully evolved Quebec farm house with its raised basement, symmetrical arrangement of door and windows, and full-length verandah, in this instance sweeping around each side of the house. What is unusual in the context of the traditional rural house in Quebec is the mansard roof. This particular kind of mansard roof – four-sided with steep upper slopes – appeared suddenly in Quebec in the latter decades of the 19th century. A characteristic and attractive Quebec feature is the uninterrupted bellcast curve at the eaves of each slope which flares out to form the roof of the verandah.

(*Canadian Inventory of Historic Building.*)

108
3525–3527 Royale Avenue, Giffard, Quebec
Constructed: ca. 1880
Material: Stone
This dwelling representing a rare combination of the so-called
Quebec artisan home with Second Empire features, indicates th
extent to which the new style penetrated vernacular building in
Quebec. Usually located on a sloping piece of property, the
artisan house is characterized by having the main living quarters
on the upper storey and a workshop or commercial area on the
ground storey. Access to the upper storey is provided in this
case by a winding metal staircase that leads to a full-length
balcony. Although this type was usually found on the Beaupré
coast east of Quebec City, it rarely appeared with a fashionable
mansard roof. The fine quality of the rough-faced masonry with
smooth ashlar trim is a tribute to the continuing fine tradition
of stone construction in Quebec.
(*Canadian Inventory of Historic Building*.)

109
Lismore
215 South Street, Cowansville, Quebec
Constructed: 1881
Material: Brick
The Eastern Townships saw the construction of a number of fine
high-style Second Empire residences during the 1870s and
1880s and Lismore, built for Cowansville mill-owner George K.
Nesbitt, is its most outstanding surviving example. The modifying
influence of a strong vernacular building tradition, which is so
often evident in Quebec's domestic architecture of the Second
Empire mode, is completely absent in this flamboyant, thor-
oughly up-to-date design. The picturesque quality of light and
shadow created by varied wall planes, pavilioned and towered
roofline, textured surfaces and abundant wood and iron ornamentation, has rarely been so fully and unabashedly exploited.
Lismore remained in the Nesbitt family until the 1950s when it
was donated to the Anglican diocese of Montreal. Since 1957 it
has served as a home for the aged known as the Nesbitt Anglican Residence.
(*Canadian Inventory of Historic Building*.)

110
Avenue de Gaspé, Saint-Jean-Port-Joli, Quebec
Constructed: ca. 1890
Architect: Charles Bernier
Material: Wood

This modest wooden house is one of several in Saint-Jean-Port-Joli which reflect the renewed popularity of the mansard roof in rural Quebec. There are other dwellings of similar design on neighbouring lots in this village, renowned for its woodworking virtuosity. This example displays a suppleness of form and carved decoration, especially in the treatment of the doorway and the graceful dormer windows. The raised basement and full-length gallery are familiar features that belong to the rural house tradition in Quebec.
(*Canadian Inventory of Historic Building*.)

111
168 Rutherford Street, Winnipeg, Manitoba
Constructed: 1881–82
Architect: L.A. Desy
Material: Brick

This is one of a pair of similar dwellings erected for partners Alexander Brown and Thomas Rutherford on the banks of the Red River adjacent to their flourishing lumber mills at Point Douglas. No. 168 Rutherford Street was built for Rutherford, No. 170 for Brown, with each man acting as his own contractor. Although neither house is enormous by Second Empire standards, being one-and-a-half storeys high and three bays wide, they nevertheless attain a sense of style through the use of the projecting central section with mansarded tower and the elliptical doorway. A contemporary account insists that they "may be classed among the handsomest buildings." While one newspaper account cites "E. Desy" as the architect, the only one residing in Winnipeg in the early 1880s was L.A. Desy, architect of the Cauchon Block (known today as the Empire Hotel).
(*Canadian Inventory of Historic Building*.)

110

112
Houlahan's Terrace
395–409 Alexander Avenue, Winnipeg, Manitoba
Constructed: 1883
Material: Brick
In 1883 a Winnipeg newspaper announced that "Mr. J. Houlahan, plasterer, has built a very fine brick terrace, three stories high and containing eight good sized houses." Houlahan's Terrace, as it came to be known, provided decent economical accommodation for working-class people including railroaders engaged at the nearby Canadian Pacific Railway yards. Though accordingly simple and unadorned, Houlahan's Terrace makes reference to the Second Empire style in its use of the mansard roof and the rhythmic series of projecting and recessing walls capped by alternating large and small conical dormers.
(*Canadian Inventory of Historic Building*.)

113
W.H. Lyon House
Graham Street, Winnipeg, Manitoba
Constructed: 1881 *Demolished:* ca. 1912
Architects: Edward McCoskrie and Joseph Greenfield
Material: Brick

The Lyon House, built for W.H. Lyon and occupied in 1883 by Dr. James Kerr, a prominent physician who had recently emigrated from Ontario, offers a good example of the gracious housing that was being produced for the well-to-do in a boom-town atmosphere. Designed by architects McCoskrie and Greenfield and built by contractors Paterson and McComb, it is a simple but substantial brick block, dressed up with ornate roof cresting and tall chimneys. The roof lantern, an unusual feature for Second Empire, and the delicate verandah are later additions carried out about 1890 for owner George Strevel under the direction of architect George Browne.

(*Public Archives Canada.*)

114

113 Princess Avenue East, Brandon, Manitoba
Constructed: ca. 1888
Material: Brick
This large yellow brick house, now subdivided into apartments,
served as a single family dwelling until the 1930s. Certain detail
recall in a vague way Second Empire prototypes. In addition to
the mansard roof, there is the attempt to articulate the wall surface through the use of bay windows and recessed panels. The
plain effect of the façade was originally relieved by a verandah
that ran across the front and down one side of the residence.
Local tradition claiming that this house was erected for barrister
and M.P.P. Clifford Sifton remains to be proven.
(*Canadian Inventory of Historic Building.*)

115
Creighton Terrace
33 Fourth Street, Emerson, Manitoba
Constructed: 1885–86
Material: Brick
Creighton Terrace was put up at the peak of Emerson's boom-
town growth, before an alternate railway route dimmed the tow
hopes of becoming the permanent gateway to western Canada
Erected by developers Noble and Fallis, the terrace was proba
bly named in honour of W.D. Creighton, part-owner of the prop
erty in the early 1880s. Conveniently located near the Red Rive
and original town core, and fitted up with a fashionable mansa
roof, this triple dwelling offered superior accommodation for
newcomers to Emerson. The first tenants to occupy Creighton
Terrace were barrister Archibald Mackay, law clerk David
Mackay and deputy postmaster and operator of the Canadian
Pacific Railway Telegraph Company, T.W. Mutchmor. Accordin
to local information, the builder was a man called Bryce.
(*Canadian Inventory of Historic Building*.)

116
Villa Laurier Hotel
9937 108th Street, Edmonton, Alberta
Demolished: ca. 1972
Material: Wood
The Villa Laurier Hotel would appear to have been built as a single family dwelling; however, since 1914 it has been used a boarding house. This is one of the few examples of residential building in the Prairies, with the exception of Winnipeg, where influence of Second Empire goes beyond the borrowing of the mansard roof. The two-storey bay windows, central tower and iron cresting indicate a more serious attempt to imitate the pure examples of this style. Perhaps its name, Villa Laurier, was cho sen to reflect the "frenchness" of its design.
(*Canadian Inventory of Historic Building*.)

117
610 Buxton Street, Indian Head, Saskatchewan
Constructed: 1890–91
Material: Stone
Erected in 1890–91 for a local farmer, Joseph Glenn, this is the only surviving stone house in Indian Head, an early western community on the main Canadian Pacific Railway line. In additio to its stone construction, the dwelling is remarkable for its flat mansard roof trimmed with gay iron cresting, so popular in the Second Empire idiom. Although no architect was apparently involved in the project, the builders have been identified as ston mason John Hunter and carpenter A.M. Fraser. The house remains the property of the Glenn family to this day.
(*Canadian Inventory of Historic Building.*)

118
1124 Fort Street, Victoria, British Columbia
Constructed: ca. 1887
Material: Wood
This substantial dwelling is one of Victoria's oldest surviving buildings. Following the trend set by contemporary buildings in the city such as the Post Office, Custom House and Public School, this house pays tribute to Second Empire fashion in such details as the mansard roof, projecting central pavilion crowned by a mansard tower and the repetition of semicircular motifs in the attic windows. The roof has regrettably lost its fish-scale shingles arranged in bands of different colours. The original owner, Thomas Joseph Jones, a native of Toronto, was one of Victoria's most successful dentists.
(*Canadian Inventory of Historic Building*.)

119

507 Head Street, Esquimalt, British Columbia

Constructed: 1893

Material: Wood

One of the most picturesque Second Empire houses on Vancouver Island, 507 Head Street bears witness to the late flowering of this fashion in the west. The house has an elaborate mansard roof with convex ribs and shaped shingles as well as two asymmetrical towers, one on the main façade, another along a lateral wall. A curious feature is the iron cresting placed above the cornice and not on top of the roof. The house was built for Captain Victor Jacobson, a sealer who anchored his schooners just off the beach in front of the property. He apparently did all the fancy carving for the roof trim himself. According to his daughter, the oak panels in the dining room, depicting flowers, animals and fish, were carved "by my father ... while waiting for seal herds to enter the Bering Sea or while his schooner was becalmed, from the patterns my mother drew."

(*Canadian Inventory of Historic Building*.)

Appendix. List of Illustrations.

1 City Hall, Montreal, Que.
2 New Louvre, Paris, France
3 Paris apartment
4 Paddington Station and Hotel, London, England
5 Design for War Office, London, England
6 City Hall, Boston
7 State War and Navy Department Building, Washington, D.C.
8 Sketches of curved roofs, France
9 French roof suburban villa
10 Toronto General Hospital, Toronto, Ont.
11, 12, 13 Parliament Buildings, Ottawa, Ont.
14 Government House, Toronto, Ont.
15 Custom House, Saint John, N.B.
16 Custom House, London, Ont.
17 Plan for Post Office, Toronto, Ont.
18 Post Office, Toronto, Ont.
19 Post Office, Ottawa, Ont.
20 Post Office, Montreal, Que.
21 Custom House, Toronto, Ont.
22 Post Office, Victoria, B.C.
23 Custom House, Victoria, B.C.
24 MacKenzie Building, Royal Military College, Kingston, Ont.
25 Post Office, Guelph, Ont.
26 Plan for Post Office, Saint-Jean, Que.
27 Plan for Post Office, Windsor, Ont.
28 Parliament Buildings, Winnipeg, Man.
29 Parliament Buildings, Quebec, Que.
30 Legislative Building, Fredericton, N.B.
31 Law Courts Building, Charlottetown, P.E.I.
32 Court House, Winnipeg, Man.
33 City Hall, Victoria, B.C.
34 City Market Building, Saint John, N.B.
35 Byward Market Building, Ottawa, Ont.
36 Falconwood Lunatic Asylum, Charlottetown, P.E.I.
37 The Athenaeum, Saint John's, Nfld
38 Masonic Temple, Victoria, B.C.
39, 40 Y.M.C.A. Building, Quebec, Que.
41 Provincial Normal School, Truro, N.S.
42 Pavillon central, Laval University, Quebec, Que.
43 Collège du Sacré-Coeur, Sorel, Que.
44 Collège Notre-Dame, Montreal, Que.
45 Saint Boniface College, Saint Boniface, Man.
46 Sacred Heart Convent, Calgary, Alta
47 Molson Bank, Montreal, Que.
48 Dominion Bank, Toronto, Ont.
49 View of Wellington Street in 1896, Ottawa, Ont.
50 Offices of the Eastern Townships Bank, P.Q.
51 Head Office of Eastern Townships Bank, Sherbrooke, Que.
52 Victoria Block, Clinton, Ont.
53 Victoria Block, Clinton, Ont.
54 Saint James Street, Montreal, Que.
55 Barron Block, Montreal, Que.
56 Odell Block, Sherbrooke, Que.
57 Commercial block, 233–237 Dundas Street, London, Ont.
58 Osler Block, Dundas, Ont.
59 Gerrie Block, Winnipeg, Man.
60 Windsor Hotel, Montreal, Que.
61 Prince of Wales Hotel, Niagara-on-the-Lake, Ont.
62 Yale Hotel, Vancouver, B.C.
63 North Street Terminal, Halifax, N.S.
64 William Bell Organ Factory, Guelph, Ont.
65 Chinic Warehouse, Quebec, Que.
66 Design for a Villa, Mount Royal, Montreal, Que.
67 House, 405 Broad Street, Dunnville, Ont.
68 Dale House, Madoc, Ont.
69 Lorne Hall, Toronto, Ont.
70 Fontbonne Hall, London, Ont.
71 Plan for Glanmore, Belleville, Ont.
72 House, 201 Charles Street, Belleville, Ont.
73 Perley House, Ottawa, Ont.
74 Wyoming, Guelph, Ont.
75 House, Hallowell Township, Ont.
76 House, 125 Rosemount Avenue, Weston, Ont.
77 House, 29 West Street, Brantford, Ont.
78 Row Housing, 332–344 Rubidge Street, Peterborough, Ont.
79 Row Housing, 119–133 Spruce Street, Toronto, Ont.
80 House, 322 Dundas Street West, Toronto, Ont.
81 Farmhouse, Maitland, N.S.
82 Quinniapiac, Saint John's, Nfld
83 House, 49 Rennies Mill Road, Saint John's, Nfld
84 House, 99 Wentworth Street, Saint John, N.B.
85 House, 354 Main Street, Saint John, N.B.
86 House, High Street, Souris East, P.E.I.
87 House, 1173 South Park Street, Halifax, N.S.
88 House, 37 Mecklenburg Street, Saint John, N.B.
89 House, 767 Brunswick Street, Fredericton, N.B.
90 Dickey House, Amherst, N.S.
91 House, 917 Loch Lomond Road, Saint John, N.B.

92 Birchwood, Charlottetown, P.E.I.
93 Queen Hotel, Annapolis Royal, N.S.
94 House, Ship Cove Road, Burin, Nfld
95 Row Housing, 176–182 Gower Street, Saint-John's, Nfld
96 House, 30 Monkstown Road, Saint John's, Nfld
97 House, 31 Lincoln Street, Lunenburg, N.S.
98 House, 143 Queen Street, Truro, N.S.
99 Shaughnessy House, Montreal, Que.
100 Row Housing, 3532–3538 Sainte-Famille Street, Montreal, Que.
101 Row Housing, 661–675 Grande Allée East, Quebec, Que.
102 Row Housing, 3837–3893 de Bullion Street, Montreal, Que.
103 House, 28 Guénette Street, Lévis, Que.
104 House, 118 Fraser Street, Rivière-du-Loup, Que.
105 House, 52 Vachon Boulevard, Sainte-Marie-de-Beauce, Que.
106 House, 7214 Royale Avenue, Château Richer, Que.
107 House, 2 Saint-Joseph Boulevard, Charlesbourg, Que.
108 House, 3525–3527 Royale Avenue, Giffard, Que.
109 Lismore, Cowansville, Que.
110 House, 189 Avenue de Gaspé, Saint-Jean-Port-Joli, Que.
111 House, 168 Rutherford Street, Winnipeg, Man.
112 Houlahan's Terrace, Winnipeg, Man.
113 Lyon House, Winnipeg, Man.
114 House, 113 Princess Avenue East, Brandon, Man.
115 Creighton Terrace, Emerson, Man.
116 Villa Laurier Hotel, Edmonton, Alta
117 House, 610 Buxton Street, Indian Head, Sask.
118 House, 1124 Fort Street, Victoria, B.C.
119 House, 507 Head Street, Esquimalt, B.C.

Endnotes

Introduction

1 The earliest appearance of the term seems to be in Rosalie Thorne McKenna, "James Renwick, Jr. and the Second Empire Style in the United States," *Magazine of Art*, Vol. 44, No. 3 (March 1951), pp. 97–101. Other major works include Eric Arthur, *Toronto No Mean City* (Toronto: University of Toronto Press, 1974), pp. 128, 171, 174; Banister Fletcher, *A History of Architecture on the Comparative Method* (London: Athlone Press, University of London, 1961), pp. 1086, 1115; Alan Gowans, *Building Canada: An Architectural History of Canadian Life* (Toronto: Oxford University Press, 1966), p. 105, Figs. 164–65, 167; R. Greenhill, K. Macpherson and D. Richardson, *Ontario Towns* (Ottawa: Oberon Press, 1974), unpaginated; Ralph W. Hammett, *Architecture in the United States: A Survey of Architectural Styles Since 1776* (New York: John Wiley & Sons, 1976), pp. 101–4; Henry-Russell Hitchcock, *Architecture: Nineteenth and Twentieth Centuries* (Harmondsworth, Middlesex: Penguin Books, 1958), pp. 131–72; Jean-Claude Marsan, *Montréal en évolution* (Montreal: Fides, 1974), pp. 224–26; Marcus Whiffen, *American Architecture Since 1780: A Guide to the Styles* (Cambridge, Mass.: M.I.T. Press, 1969), pp. 102–8.

2 *Canadian Illustrated News* (Montreal), 5 March 1870, p. 282; 16 Nov. 1872, p. 316; 2 June 1877, p. 342; 2 Feb. 1878, p. 79.

3 Canada. *General Report of the Minister of Public Works for the Year Ending 30 June, 1873* (Ottawa: Queen's Printer, 1874), pp. 40, 122–25, 128, 131; Canada. *General Report of the Minister of Public Works for the Year Ending 30 June, 1879* (Ottawa: Queen's Printer, 1880), p. 15; Canada. *General Report of the Minister of Public Works for the Year Ending 30 June, 1881* (Ottawa: Queen's Printer, 1882), p. 25; Canada. *General Report of the Minister of Public Works from 30 June, 1867, to 1st July, 1882* (Ottawa: Queen's Printer, 1883), pp. 148, 152–53, 173, 181, 194.

4 Samuel Sloan, *Sloan's Homestead Architecture, Containing Forty Designs for Villas, Cottages, and Farmhouses, with Essays on Style, Construction, Landscape Gardening, Furniture, etc., etc.* (Philadelphia: J.B. Lippincott & Company, 1861), design XXXI; George Evertson Woodward, *Woodward's National Architect* (New York: Geo. E. Woodward, ca. 1869), Nos. 2, 17; Isaac H. Hobbs and Son, *Hobbs's Architecture: Containing Designs and Ground Plans for Villas, Cottages and other Edifices, both Suburban and Rural* (Philadelphia: J.B. Lippincott & Co., 1873), pp. 34, 38, 66; Elisha Charles Hussey, *Home Building. A Reliable Book of Facts, relating to Building, Living, Materials, Costs* (New York: Leader & Van Hoesen, ca. 1876), Figs. 17, 29.

5 Boston. Committee on Public Buildings, *The City Hall, Boston* (Boston: City Council, 1866), p. v.

6 John W. Kennion, *The Architects' and Builders' Guide* (New York: Fitzpatrick & Hunter, 1868), p. 57.

7 Ibid., p. 49.

Montreal City Hall: A Classic Canadian Example

1 Apparently there was a structural difference between the mansard roof in France and its North American counterpart. Commenting on a recent fire in Boston, a "Frenchman" indignantly wrote to the *New York Herald*, "In your discussions on mansard roofs please take notice that American mansard roofs are not French mansard roofs. The mansard roof, so called in America, could not be built in any portion of France, as it is a fraud and a scandal. The mansard roof of France is always fireproof, being built in accordance with French law of, iron, brick and mortar. When American architects cease to foist upon credulous real estate owners their cheap frauds you may expect a cessation of the punishment Boston has just received during the past few days" (*Quebec Gazette*, 20 Nov. 1872), p. [2].

2 A. Leblond de Brumath, *Guide de Montréal et de ses environs* (Montreal: Granger Frères, 1897), p. 63.

Second Empire and Napoleon III of France

1 J.S. Ingram, *The Centennial Exposition Described and Illustrated* (Philadelphia: Hubbard Bros., ca. 1876), p. 40.

2 Geoffrey de Bellaigue, "Queen Victoria Buys French in 1855," *The Antique Collector*, Vol. 46, No. 4 (April 1975), pp. 37–41.

3 These wide boulevards also served a military purpose, for they permitted easy penetration of troops into the city centre in case of civil unrest.

4 Sanford E. Loring, *Principles and Practices of Architecture* (Chicago: Cobb, Pritchard and Co., 1869), p. 42.

5 Henry-Russell Hitchcock, *Architecture: Nineteenth and Twentieth Centuries* (Harmondsworth, Middlesex: Penguin Books, 1958), p. 135.

England: Early Advocate of Second Empire

1 Henry-Russell Hitchcock, "Second Empire *avant la lettre*," *La Gazette des Beaux-Arts*, Vol. 42 ([Aug.]1953), pp. 118, 124–26.

2 Ibid., p. 125.

3 Boston, Committee on Public Buildings, loc. cit.

Second Empire and the United States

1 Boston, Committee on Public Buildings, op. cit. pp. iv–v.

2 Marcus Whiffen, op. cit., p. 103.

3 Lawrence Wodehouse, "Alfred B. Mullett and his French style Government Buildings," *Journal of the Society of Architectural Historians*, Vol. 31, No. 1 (March 1972), pp. 22–37. Hitchcock has claimed that Gilman, architect of the Boston City Hall, was the real source of these Second Empire designs, for Gilman also worked for the Treasury Department (Henry-Russell Hitchcock, *Architecture: Nineteenth and Twentieth Centuries* [Harmondsworth, Middlesex: Penguin Books, 1958], p. 168).

4 Calvert Vaux, *Villas and Cottages* (New York: Harper & Brothers, 1857), p. 54.

5 Ibid., p. 90.

6 Henry Hudson Holly, *Holly's Country Seats* (New York: D. Appleton & Company, 1863), p. 149.

7 George L. Hersey, "Godey's Choice," *Journal of the Society of Architectural Historians*, Vol. 18, No. 3 (Oct. 1959), p. 104.

8 Isaac Hobbs and Son, op. cit., n.p.

9 Pattern books with the highest concentration of Second Empire designs include Gilbert Bostwick Croff, *Model Suburban Architecture Embodying Designs for Dwellings of Moderate Cost* (New York: Roby & O'Neil [1870]) and *Progressive American Architecture* (New York: Orange Judd & Company [1875]); Marcus F. Cummings, *Cummings' Architectural Details* (New York: Orange Judd & Company, 1873); Marcus F. Cummings and Charles Crosby Miller, *Modern American Architecture* (Troy, N.Y.: The authors, 1868); Isaac Hobbs and Son, op. cit.; George E. Woodward, op. cit.

Canada; Stirrings of Second Empire

1 Canada. Public Archives (hereafter cited as PAC), RG 11 Vol. 841, exhibits 62–63, p. 7. This manuscript proposal by "Semper Paratus", code name for Fuller and Jones, accompanied their competition plans of 1859. The authors are grateful to Professor D.S. Richardson for bringing this proposal to their attention.
2 Ibid.
3 *Canadian Illustrated News* (Montreal), 19 Oct. 1872, p. 245.

Department of Public Works

1 *Daily Telegraph* (Saint John), 26 April 1881, pp. 1–2.
2 Ibid.

Commercial Building

1 *The Dominion Guide* (Montreal), 7 June 1873, p. 354.

Conclusions

1 Palliser, Palliser & Co., architects, *Palliser's New Cottage Homes and Details* (New York: Palliser, Palliser & Co. [ca. 1887]), n.p. [introduction].
2 *Horrors in Architecture and So-called Works of Art in Bronze in the City of New York ... By an Admirer of Art Whose Name is of no Consequence to the Reader* (New York: n.p., 1886), p. 4.
3 Eugene Clarence Gardner, *The House that Jill Built, After Jack's Had Proved a Failure* (New York: Fords, Howard & Hulbert, 1882), pp. 113–14.

Legend Sources

1 Luc d'Iberville-Moreau, *Lost Montreal* (Toronto: Oxford University Press, 1975), p. 107; Jean-Claude Marsan, *Montréal en évolution* (Montreal: Fides, 1974), pp. 204, 224–25.
2 Henry Bidou, *Paris*, trans. J. Lewis May (London: Johnathan Cape, 1939), p. 399; Henry-Russell Hitchcock, *Architecture: Nineteenth and Twentieth Centuries* (Harmondsworth, Middlesex: Penguin Books, 1958), pp. 133–35; David H. Pinkney, *Napoleon III and the Rebuilding of Paris* (Princeton, N.J.: Princeton University Press, 1958), pp. 80–81.
3 Sanford E. Loring, *Principles and Practices of Architecture* (Chicago, Cleveland: Cobb, Pritchard and Company, 1869), pp. 42–45; David H. Pinkney, op. cit., pp. 91–92.
4 Henry-Russell Hitchcock, *Architecture: Nineteenth and Twentieth Centuries* (Harmondsworth, Middlesex: Penguin Books, 1958), p. 159; Ibid., "Second Empire *avant la lettre*'," *La Gazette des Beaux-Arts*, Vol. 42 ([Aug.] 1953), p. 124.
5 Henry-Russell Hitchcock, *Architecture: Nineteenth and Twentieth Centuries* (Harmondsworth, Middlesex: Penguin Books, 1958), p. 159.
6 Boston. Committee on Public Buildings, *The City Hall, Boston* (Boston: City Council, 1866); Ralph W. Hammett, *Architecture in the United States: A Survey of Architectural Styles Since 1776* (New York: John Wiley & Sons, 1976), pp. 101–2; Henry-Russell Hitchcock, *Architecture: Nineteenth and Twentieth Centuries* (Harmondsworth, Middlesex: Penguin Books, 1958), pp. 167–68.
7 Alan Gowans, *Images of American Living; Four Centuries of Architecture and Furniture as Cultural Expression* (Philadelphia: J.B. Lippincott, 1964), p. 30; Henry-Russell Hitchcock, *Architecture: Nineteenth and Twentieth Centuries* (Harmondsworth, Middlesex: Penguin Books, 1958), p. 169; Lawrence Wodehouse, "Alfred B. Mullett and his French Style Government Buildings," *Journal of the Society of Architectural Historians*, Vol. 31, No. 1 (March 1972), pp. 22–37.
8 Calvert Vaux, *Villas and Cottages* (New York: Harper & Brothers, 1857), p. 54.
9 George L. Hersey, "Godey's Choice," *Journal of the Society of Architectural Historians*, Vol. 18, No. 3 (Oct. 1959), pp. 104–11; Isaac H. Hobbs and Son, *Hobbs's Architecture: Containing Designs and Ground Plans for Villas, Cottages and other Edifices, both Suburban and Rural* (Philadelphia: J.B. Lippincott & Company, 1873), pp. 13, 17, 21.
10 Eric Arthur, *Toronto No Mean City* (Toronto: University of Toronto Press, 1974), pp. 114–16.
11, 12, 13 PAC, RG 11, Vol. 841, exhibits 62–63, p. 4; Courtney C.J. Bond, *City on the Ottawa* (Ottawa: Queen's Printer, 1961), pp. 122–25; Douglas Richardson, "The Spirit of the Place," *Canadian Antiques Collector*, Vol. 10, No. 5 (Sept.–Oct. 1975), pp. 27–29.
14 "Residence of the Lieut.-Governor of Ontario, Canada," *Canadian Illustrated News* (Montreal), 5 March 1870, p. 282; Toronto. Metropolitan Toronto Library Board, Canadiana and Manuscripts Section, File on Government House.
15 Canada. Department of Public Works, *Annual Report of the Minister of Public Works for the Fiscal Year Ending 30 June 1879* (Ottawa: Queen's Printer, 1880), p. 15; "The Saint John Custom House," *Daily Telegraph* (Saint John), 26 April 1881, pp. [1–2].

16 Canada. Department of Public Works, *General Report of the Minister of Public Works for the Fiscal Year Ending 30 June 1873* (Ottawa: Queen's Printer, 1874), App. 18, p. 123; PAC, RG11, Vol. 3919, Specifications for addition to Custom House, London, p. 1; Association of Ontario Land Surveyors, "William Robinson," in *Annual Report of the Association of Ontario Land Surveyors* (Toronto: 1915), No. 30, pp. 51–52.

17, 18 Eric Arthur C.J. Bond, op. cit., pp. 126–27; Canada. Department of Public Works, *General Report of the Minister of Public Works for the Fiscal Year Ending 30 June 1873* (Ottawa: Queen's Printer, 1874), App. 18, pp. 124–25; PAC, RG 11, Vol. 309, Subject 881, pp. 941–45, John Dewe to Department of Public Works, Toronto, 4 March 1870; PAC, RG 11, Vol. 314, subject 884, p. 266, F.P. Rubidge to T. Trudeau, Toronto, 24 Oct. 1870.

19 Courtney C.J. Bond, *City on the Ottawa* (Ottawa: Queen's Printer, 1961), p. 15; Canada. Department of Public Works, *General Report of the Minister of Public Works for the Fiscal Year Ending 30 June 1873* (Ottawa: Queen's Printer, 1874), App. 18, p. 122; PAC, RG 11, Vol. 291, subject 801, p. 82, T.S. Scott to F. Braum, Ottawa, 27 July 1871.

20 Canada. Department of Public Works, *General Report of the Minister of Public Works for the Fiscal Year Ending 30 June 1873* (Ottawa: Queen's Printer, 1874), App. 18, pp. 127–28; Jean-Claude Marsan, *Montréal en évolution* (Montreal: Fides, 1974), p. 225.

21 Canada. Department of Public Works, *General Report of the Minister of Public Works for the Fiscal Year Ending 30 June 1873* (Ottawa: Queen's Printer, 1874), App. 18, p. 125; C. Pelham Mulvany, *Toronto: Past and Present* (Toronto: W.E. Caiger, 1884), p. 51.

22 Canada. Department of Public Works, *General Report of the Minister of Public Works for the Fiscal Year Ending 30 June 1874* (Ottawa: Queen's Printer, 1875), App. 19, p. 129; PAC, RG 11, Vol. 364, subject 993, p. 674, Benjamin W. Pearse to F. Braum, Victoria, 11 March 1873.

23 Canada. Department of Public Works, *General Report of the Minister of Public Works for the Fiscal Year Ending 30 June 1874* (Ottawa: Queen's Printer, 1875), App. 19, p. 129; John Crosby Freeman, "The Other Victoria," *Revue d'art canadienne/Canadian Art Review*, Vol. 1, No. 1 (1974), p. 39; G. Edward Mills, "1002 Wharf Street, Custom House: Victoria: CIHB Report," manuscript on file, National Historic Parks and Sites Branch, Parks Canada, Ottawa, 1976.

24 Canada. Department of Public Works, *General Report of the Minister of Public Works for the Fiscal Year Ending 30 June 1877* (Ottawa: Queen's Printer, 1878), App. 16, p. 73; Alan Gowans, *Building Canada: An Architectural History of Canadian Life* (Toronto: Oxford University Press, 1966), p. 142; Richard Arthur Preston, *Canada's RMC: A History of the Royal Military College* (Toronto: University of Toronto Press, 1969), p. 60.

25 Canada. Department of Public Works, *General Report of the Minister of Public Works for the Fiscal Year Ending 30 June 1876* (Ottawa: Queen's Printer, 1877), App. 17, pp. 79–80.

26 Canada. Department of Public Works, *Annual Report of the Minister of Public Works for the Fiscal Year Ending 30 June l878* (Ottawa: Queen's Printer, 1879), App. 15, p. 77; *General Report of the Minister of Public Works from 30 June 1867 to 30 June 1882* (Ottawa: Queen's Printer, 1883), Vol. I, p. 169.

27 Canada. Department of Public Works, *Annual Report of the Minister of Public Works for the Fiscal Year Ending 30 June 1879* (Ottawa: Queen's Printer, 1880), App. 3, p. 12.

28 Canada. Department of Public Works, *Annual Report of the Minister of Public Works for the Fiscal Year Ending 30 June 1881* (Ottawa: Queen's Printer, 1882), pp. 25–26; "The Building Boom," *Winnipeg Daily Sun*, 20 Oct. 1883, p. 2.

29 A.J.H. Richardson, "Guide to the Architecturally and Historically most Significant Buildings in the Old City of Quebec," *Bulletin of the Association for Preservation Technology*, Vol. 2, Nos. 3–4 (1970), pp. 56–57; Gérard Morisset, "Le Parlement de Québec," *Habitat*, Vol. 3, No. 6 (Nov.–Dec. 1966), pp. 25–28; James M. Lemoine, *Picturesque Quebec* (Montreal: Dawson Brothers, 1882), pp. 255–57; Luc Noppen, "L'architecture des parlements de Québec," *L'Action* (Québec), 21 April 1973.

30 "The New Buildings," *New Brunswick Reporter* (Fredericton), 31 March 1880, p. [2]; C. Anne Hale, "The Legislative Building, 750 Queen Street, Fredericton: CIHB Report," manuscript on file, National Historic Parks and Sites Branch, Parks Canada, Ottawa, 1974.

31 Irene Rogers, "Law Courts Building, Charlottetown: CIHB Report," manuscript on file, National Historic Parks and Sites Branch, Parks Canada, Ottawa, 1974; J.H. Meacham & Co., *Illustrated Historical Atlas of Prince Edward Island* (1880; reprint ed., Belleville, Ont.: Mika Silk Screening Ltd., 1972), p. 27.

32 Vancouver Daily World, *Illustrated Souvenir Publication* (Vancouver: Vancouver Daily World, 1891), pp. 22–23; Randy R. Rostecki, "Law Courts Building, 391 Broadway, Winnipeg: CIHB Report," manuscript on file, National Historic Parks and Sites and Branch, Parks Canada, Ottawa, 1976; *Daily Telegraph* (Saint John, N.B.), 2 Oct. 1878, p. 3; "The Old and The New: Provincial Court House and Jail," *Winnipeg Daily Sun*, 20 Jan. 1883, p. 8; "The Building Boom," *Winnipeg Daily Sun*, 20 Oct. 1883, p. 2.

33 City of Victoria Heritage Advisory Committee, *City of Victoria* (Victoria: 1974), p. 18; William Cochrane, ed., *The Canadian Album: Men of Canada* (Brantford, Ont.: Bradley, Carretson, 1891), p. 114; John Crosby Freeman, "The Other Victoria," *Revue d'art canadienne/Candian Art Review*, Vol. 1, No. 1 (1974), pp. 38–39; G. Edward Mills and Janet Wright, "Victoria City Hall: Screening Paper," manuscript on file, National Historic Parks and Sites Branch, Parks Canada, Ottawa, 1977.

34 C. Anne Hale, "City Market Building, 47 Charlotte Street, Saint John: CIHB Report," manuscript on file, National Historic Parks and Sites Branch, Parks Canada, Ottawa, 1974; Staff Report, "City Market Building, Saint John: Screening Paper," manuscript on file, National Historic Parks and Sites Branch, Parks Canada, 1970.

35 Lucien Brault, *Ottawa Old and New* (Ottawa: Historical Information Institute, 1946), p. 107; Ottawa. Municipal Archives, Minutes of Council for part of the years 1874, 1875, 1876 and 1877, pp. 185–86, 200.

36 Henry M. Hurd, ed., *The Institutional Care of the Insane in the United States and Canada* (New York: Arno Press, 1973), Vol. 4, pp. 211–15; "L'asile d'alienés de Falconwood," *L'Opinion publique* (Montreal), 23 March 1873, p. 146; Prince Edward Island. House of Assembly, *Journal of the House of Assembly, 1878* (Charlottetown: Queen's Printer, 1878), App. E, p. A.

37 Joseph R. Smallwood, ed., *The Book of Newfoundland* (St. John's: Newfoundland Book Publishers, 1967), Vol. 4, pp. 190–91; "Laying Foundation Stone of Athenaeum," *Royal Gazette and Newfoundland Advertiser* (St. John's), 9 Nov. 1875, p. [2].

38 G. Edward Mills, "Masonic Temple, Victoria: CIHB Report," manuscript on file, National Historic Parks and Sites Branch, Parks Canada, Ottawa, 1975.

39, 40 Christina Cameron, "950–964 Saint-Jean Street, Quebec: CIHB Report," manuscript on file, National Historic Parks and Sites Branch, Parks Canada, Ottawa, 1972; Québec. Archives civiles de Québec, greffe W. Bignell, Contract between John Hatch and the Y.M.C.A., Quebec, 21 Jan. 1979, No. 9653.

41 Nova Scotia. House of Assembly, *Journals of the House of Assembly* (Halifax: Queen's Printer, 1878), App. 1, p. 35; Ibid. (Halifax: Queen's Printer, 1879), App. 5, p. xx; *Truro, Nova Scotia: The Hub of the Province* (Grand Rapids, Mich.: James Bayne, n.d.), n.p.

42 A.J.H. Richardson, "Guide to the Architecturally and Historically most Significant Buildings in the Old City of Quebec," *Bulletin of the Association for Preservation Technology*, Vol. 2, Nos. 3–4 (1970), pp. 64–65; Québec. Archives du Séminaire de Québec, Journal du Séminaire, Vol. 2, 31 May 1875, 21 Oct. 1876.

43 Abbé A. Couillard-Després, *Histoire de Sorel* (Montreal: Imprimerie des sourds-muets, 1926), pp. 242–55.

44 Montreal. Archives du collège Notre-Dame, Journal du collège; Charles P. De Volpi and P.S. Winkworth, *Montreal: Recueil iconographique/A Pictorial Record*, Vol. 2 (Montreal: Dev-Sco Publications, 1963), p. 299.

45 Dom Benoit, *Vie de Mgr Taché* (Montreal: Librairie Beauchemin, 1904), Vol. 2, pp. 374–76, 497–98; Randy R. Rostecki, unpublished research notes on Saint Boniface College, Sept. 1977; "Reopening of Saint John's Church," *Saint John Daily News* (N.B.), 25 Nov. 1872, p. [3]; "The Bull's Eye: Great Growth of Winnipeg," *Winnipeg Daily Sun*, 30 Oct. 1883, p. 3; the authors wish to thank Lionel Dorge of the archbishopric of Saint Boniface, Manitoba, for his generous assistance in researching this building.

46 Calgary. Sacred Heart Convent, Annals of the Sisters, Faithful Companions of Jesus, 1893, the authors are grateful to Sister Gabriel Cummins, F.C.J. for relaying this information; Douglas Coats, "Calgary: The Private Schools, 1900–16," in *Frontier Calgary*, ed. A.W. Rasporich and H.C. Klassen (Calgary: University of Calgary, McClelland and Stewart West, 1975), p. 144.

47 Phyllis Lambert and Robert Lemire, *Inventaire des bâtiments du vieux Montréal, du quartier Saint-Antoine et de la ville de Maisonneuve construits entre 1880 et 1915* (Québec: Ministère des Affaires culturelles, 1977), dossier 25, p. 25; A.J.H. Richardson, "Guide to the Architecturally and Historically most Significant Buildings in the Old City of Quebec," *Bulletin of the Association for Preservation Technology*, Vol. 2, Nos. 3–4 (1970), pp. 76–77; J. Douglas Stewart, "Architecture for a Boom Town: The Primitive and the Neo-Baroque in George Browne's Kingston Buildings," in *To Preserve and Defend: Essays on Kingston in the Nineteenth Century*, ed. Gerald Tulchinsky (Montreal: McGill-Queen's University Press, 1976), p. 37.

48 Anne Little, Department of Economic Research, Toronto Dominion Bank, Toronto, to Janet Wright, personal communication on the Dominion Bank, 13 Sept. 1977; Joseph Schull, *100 Years of Banking: A History of the Toronto Dominion Bank* (Toronto: Copp Clark, 1958), p. 65.

49 Charles E. Goad, *Insurance Atlas of the City of Ottawa* (Toronto: Charles E. Goad, rev. ed. 1895), Pl. 35; *Dominion Illustrated* (Montreal), "A Word from Wellington Street," 21 July 1888, p. 35; id., "Special number devoted to Ottawa and the Parliament Buildings of Canada" (Montreal: Sabiston Litho. and Publishing Co., 1981), pp. 128–29.

50 Eastern Townships Bank, *Charter and Annual Reports, 1859–1912* (Sherbrooke: 1912), pp. 128–29, 138, 149, 161, 456.

51 Ibid., pp. 138–39, 149, 161, 404; "Local and Other Items," *Gazette* (Sherbrooke), 9 April 1875, p. [3]; Victor Ross, *The History of the Canadian Bank of Commerce* (Toronto: Oxford University Press, 1920), Vol. 1, p. 365.

52, 53 *New Era* (Clinton, Ont.), 24 Jan. 1878, n.p.; the authors are grateful to Mr. Gerald Fremlin of Clinton, Ontario, for his assistance in researching this building.

54 Charles E. Goad, *Atlas of the City of Montreal* (Toronto, Montreal: Charles E. Goad, 1881), Pl. III; *Lovell's Montreal Directory* (Montreal: John Lovell, 1873), p. 202.

55 "Barron Block," *Canadian Illustrated News* (Montreal), 27 Aug. 1870, p. 130; "Le Bloc Barron," *L'Opinion publique* (Montreal), 4 July 1872, pp. 316, 320.

56 Marie-Jeanne Daigneau, archivist, Société d'histoire des Cantons de l'Est, Sherbrooke, Quebec, unpublished research on the Odell Block, Nov. 1977; "The Metropolis of the Eastern Townships," *Dominion Illustrated* (Montreal), 30 Aug. 1890, pp. 134, 149; PAC, National Map Collection, H2/340–Sherbrooke–1881, Bird's eye view of Sherbrooke, P.Q., 1881.

57 John Lutman and John Picur, unpublished research notes on 233–237 Dundas Street compiled for the Local Advisory Committee on Architectural Conservation, London, Ontario, 1977.

58 Dundas Historical Society Museum, unpublished research notes on 5–7 Main Street, Dundas, Ontario, Oct. 1977; Page and Smith, *Illustrated Historical Atlas of the County of Wentworth, Ontario* (reprint of 1875 ed., Dundas, Ontario: Dundas Valley School of Art, 1971), pp. xviii, xxxvi, 59.

59 Randy R. Rostecki, "The Rise and Demise of Winnipeg's Central Business District," manuscript on file, National Historic Parks and Sites Branch, Parks Canada, Ottawa, 1976, pp. 3–4, 8; W.D. Steen and E.E. Boyce, *Winnipeg, Manitoba and her Industries* (Winnipeg: Steen and Boyce, 1882), pp. 31–32.

60 Lady Dufferin, *My Canadian Journal 1872–1878*, ed. Gladys Chantler Walker (Don Mills, Ontario: Longmans Canada, 1969), p. 283; *Gazette* (Montreal), 29 Jan. 1878, p. 2; Edwin C. Guillet, *Pioneer Inns and Taverns* (Toronto: Ontario Publishing, 1956), Vol. 2, pp. 109–12; "Opening of New Windsor Hotel," *Daily Witness* (Montreal) 28 Jan. 1878, p. 8; "Vice-Regal Visit to Montreal," *Canadian Illustrated News* (Montreal), 23 Feb. 1878, pp. 119, 121; "The Windsor Hotel," "The Vice-Regal Visit," *Daily Witness* (Montreal), 15 Feb. 1878, p. 4; Henry F. Withey and Elsie R. Withey, *Biographical Dictionary of American Architects (Deceased)* (Los Angeles: New Age Publishing Company, 1956), p. 71.

61 David Flemming, *A History of the Town of Niagara-on-the-Lake (1791–1970)*, Manuscript Report Series No. 25 (Ottawa: Parks Canada, 1971), p. 75; Niagara County Historical Museum, Niagara-on-the-Lake, Ontario, unpublished research on the Prince of Wales Hotel, Sept. 1977; *Niagara-on-the-Lake, Canada* (Niagara-on-the-Lake: Town Council of Niagara-on-the-Lake, n.d.), p. 27.

62 Harold Kalman, *Exploring Vancouver* (Vancouver: University of British Columbia Press, 1974), pp. 153, 156; Donald Kerr, "Vancouver – A Study in Human Geography," MA thesis, University of Toronto, Toronto, 1943, p. 43; Warren Sommer, "Yale Hotel, Vancouver: CIHB Report," manuscript on file, National Historic Parks and Sites Branch, Parks Canada, Ottawa, 1975.

63 "The New Intercolonial Railway Depot," *Daily Acadian Recorder* (Halifax), 28 July 1877, p. [1]; Canada. Department of Public Works, *General Report of the Minister of Public Works for the Fiscal Year Ending 30 June 1878* (Ottawa: Queen's Printer, 1878), App. 21, pp. 167–68; PAC, RG 12, Vol. 1913, File No. 3316–5, Specifications for a Passenger Terminal, Halifax N.S., 23 Oct. 1874; W.H. Howard, *Halifax of Today: An Illustrated Souvenir of the Queen's Diamond Jubilee, 1837–97* (Halifax: W.H. Howard, 1897), p. 23; Mathilde Brosseau and David McConnell, "The Stations of the Intercolonial Railway, 1867–1914: Screening Paper," manuscript on file, National Historic Parks and Sites Branch, Parks Canada, Ottawa, 1974, pp. 5, 13–15.

64 Gordon R. Couling, unpublished research notes on William Bell Organ Factory, Guelph, Ontario, May 1977; Historical Atlas Publishing Company, *Historical Atlas of Wellington County* (1906; reprint ed., Wellington County: Corporation of the County of Wellington, 1972), p. 14.

65 Christina Cameron, "47 Dalhousie Street, Quebec: CIHB Report," manuscript on file, National Historic Parks and Sites Branch, Parks Canada, Ottawa, 1972.

66 Gilbert Bostwick Croff, *Model Suburban Architecture, Embodying Designs for Dwellings of Moderate Cost* (New York: Roby & O'Neil [1870]); *Progressive American Architecture* (New York: Orange Judd & Company [1875]); C. Anne Hale, "Report on D.E. Dunham," manuscript on file, National Historic Parks and Sites Branch, Parks Canada, Ottawa, 1974, p. 10.

67 James Dickhout, unpublished research notes on 405 Broad Street West, Dunnville, Ontario, Nov. 1977; *Ontario Gazetteer and Business Directory* (Toronto: R.L. Polk, 1888–89), p. 324.

68 Madoc Review, *Way Back When* (Madoc: Pigden and McKinnon, 1976), pp. 72–73; the authors are grateful to Mr. Martin Lewis and the Hastings County Museum in Belleville for their assistance in researching this building.

69 *City Directory of Toronto* (Toronto: Might Directories, 1889–1976), title varies; William Davies, *Letters of William Davies, 1854–61*, ed. William Sherwood Fox (Toronto: University of Toronto Press, 1945), pp. 3, 133, 140; Charles E. Goad, *Atlas of the City of Toronto* (Montreal: Charles E. Goad, 1884), Pl. 31; Toronto. Toronto Historical Board, File on 3 Meredith Crescent, Toronto.

70 John Lutman, "534 Queens Avenue, London: CIHB Report," manuscript on file, National Historic Parks and Sites Branch, Parks Canada, Ottawa, 1977.

71 Mr. and Mrs. N.H. Mika, "Phillips-Faulkner House, Belleville: Screening Paper," 1969; John Witham, "Research notes on Thomas Hanley: CIHB," 1973, manuscripts on file, National Historic Parks and Sites Branch, Parks Canada, Ottawa.

72 Lois Foster, unpublished research notes on 201 Charles Street, Belleville, compiled for the Hastings County Historical Society, Belleville, July 1977.

73 *Ottawa Directory and Dominion Guide* (Ottawa: A.S. Woodburn, 1875), p. 70.

74 "Goldie Home Sold: Fine Residence Changes Hands," *Mercury* (Guelph, Ont.), June 1952, n.p.; "110-Year-Old Guelph Home," *Mercury* (Guelph, Ont.), 20 March 1976, n.p.; the authors would like to thank Gordon R. Couling of Guelph, Ontario for his kind assistance in researching this building.

77 PAC, National Map Collection, H3/440–Brantford–[1875], Bird's eye view of Brantford, Ontario, drawn by H. Brosius, Chas. Schoder, Prop's Chicago Lith., 1875.

78 Martha Ann Kidd, unpublished research notes on 332–344 Rubidge Street, Peterborough, Ontario, Sept. 1977; Randy R. Rostecki, unpublished research notes on terrace block on Edmonton Street, Winnipeg, Manitoba, Sept. 1977.

79 *Toronto City Directory* (Toronto: R.L. Polk Directories, 1887–88).

80 Ibid.

82 Allison Earle, "Quinniapiac, 25 Winter Avenue, Saint John's: CIHB Report," manuscript on file, National Historic Parks and Sites Branch, Parks Canada, Ottawa, 1974.

83 Allison Earle, "49 Rennies Mill Road, Saint John's, Newfoundland: CIHB Report," manuscript on file, National Historic Parks and Sites Branch, Parks Canada, Ottawa, 1974; "A $20,000 Residence: Mr. Marshall's Magnificent Cottage," *Evening Telegram* (Saint John's, Nfld), 23 March 1885, p. 2.

84 C. Anne Hale, "Report on D.E. Dunham," p. 10; "99 Wentworth Street, Saint John: CIHB Report," manuscripts on file, National Historic Parks and Sites Branch, Parks Canada, Ottawa, 1974; "A Handsome French Cottage," *Daily Telegraph* (Saint John, N.B.), 14 Nov. 1877, p. [3].

85 C. Anne Hale, "354 Main Street, Saint John: CIHB Report," manuscript on file, National Historic Parks and Sites Branch, Parks Canada, Ottawa, 1974; David Russell Jack, "Book Plates," *Acadiensis*, Vol. 1, No. 2 (April 1901), pp. 96–97. St. John, N.B.

86 J.H. Meacham & Co., *Illustrated Historical Atlas of Prince Edward Island* (1880; reprint ed., Belleville, Ont.: Mika Silk Screening Ltd., 1972), pp. 157–58.

87 Phyliss R. Blakeley, *Glimpses of Halifax* (Halifax: Public Archives of Nova Scotia, 1949), p. 99; *McAlpine's Halifax City Directory* (Halifax: McAlpine's Directories, 1887–88, 1895–96).

88 Russel H. Conwell, *History of the Great Fire of St. John, June 20 and 21, 1877* (Boston: B.B. Russell, 1877), p. 207; PAC, National Map Collection, H3/240–St. John–[1882], Bird's eye view of St. John, New Brunswick, O.H. Bailey, 1882.

89 C. Anne Hale, "767 Brunswick Street, Fredericton: CIHB Report," manuscript on file, National Historic Parks and Sites Branch, Parks Canada, Ottawa, 1974.

92 *Examiner* (Charlottetown), 2 June 1877, n.p.; Irene Rogers, "Birchwood, 35 Longworth Avenue, Charlottetown: CIHB Report," manuscript on file, National Historic Parks and Sites Branch, Parks Canada, Ottawa, 1974.

93 *Mirror* (Digby, N.S.), 13 July 1977, p. 2.

96 Newfoundland Historic Trust, *A Gift of Heritage: Historic Architecture of St. John's* (St. John's: Newfoundland Historic Trust Publications, 1975), Vol. 1, p. 23; Shane O'Dea, *The Domestic Architecture of Old St. John's* (St. John's: Newfoundland Historical Society, 1974), Pamphlet No. 2, pp. [16–19].

98 *Truro, Nova Scotia: The Hub of the Province* (Grand Rapids, Michigan: James Bayne, 18–), p. 19.

99 Montreal. Archives nationales du Québec, greffe C. Cushing, building contract between Robert Brown and Charles Lamontagne, 3 Feb. 1874, building contract between Robert Brown and Edward Maxwell, 3 Feb. 1874, building contract between Duncan McIntyre and Edward Maxwell, 3 Feb. 1874; "Shaughnessy House, 1923 Dorchester Street West, Montreal: Screening Paper," manuscript on file, National Historic Parks and Sites Branch, Parks Canada, Ottawa, 1973.

00 André Giroux, "3532–3538 Sainte-Famille Street, Montreal: CIHB Report," manuscript on file, National Historic Parks and Sites Branch, Parks Canada, Ottawa, 1972; Charles E. Goad, *Atlas of the City of Montreal* (Montreal: Charles E. Goad, 1881), Pl. VIII; *Lovell's Montreal Directory* (Montreal: John Lovell, 1872–78).

01 E.C. Woodley, *The House of Joseph in the Life of Quebec* (Quebec: n.p., 1946), pp. 54, 56, 68, 74; Quebec. Archives civiles, greffe P. Huot, marché between Abraham Joseph and William McDonald, 9 June 1882, No. 8694, marché between Abraham Joseph and John O'Leary, 10 June 1882, No. 8697, marché between Abraham Joseph and Joseph Garneau, 10 June 1882, No. 8698, marché between Abraham Joseph and Zepherin Vaudry, 10 June 1882, No. 8699; *Quebec City Directory* (Quebec, 1882–1930), title and publisher vary.

02 Charles E. Goad, *Atlas of the City of Montreal* (Montreal: Charles E. Goad, 1881), Pl. XXX; *Lovell's Montreal Directory* (Montreal: John Lovell, 1874–82).

03 *Quebec City Directory* (Quebec, 1889–1918), Publisher varies.

05 The authors are grateful to Maître Jean Perchat, notaire, Sainte-Marie-de-Beauce, for his kind assistance in researching this dwelling.

09 Iris Moffat, matron of the Nesbitt Anglican Residence, Cowansville, unpublished research, Nov. 1977.

10 Simon Fortin, geneological historian, Saint-Jean-Port-Joli, Quebec.

11 "The Building Boom," *Manitoba Free Press* (Winnipeg), 12 April 1881, p. 1; Randy R. Rostecki, unpublished research notes on 168 Rutherford Street, Winnipeg, Manitoba, Aug. 1977.

12 Ivan Saunders, "395–409 Alexander Avenue, Winnipeg: CIHB Report," manuscript on file, National Historic Parks and Sites Branch, Parks Canada, Ottawa, 1974; "The Building Boom," *Winnipeg Daily Sun*, 20 Oct. 1883, p. 3.

113 *Henderson's Directory of the City of Winnipeg* (Winnipeg: James Henderson, 1880–1912); R. Mitchell and T.K. Thorlakson, "James Kerr, 1848–1911, and Henry Hyland Kerr, 1881–1963; Pioneer Canadian-American Surgeons," *Canadian Journal of Surgery*, Vol. 9 (July 1966), pp. 213–20; Randy R. Rostecki, unpublished research notes on W.H. Lyon house, Winnipeg, Manitoba, Aug. 1977; "The Building Boom," *Manitoba Free Press* (Winnipeg), 12 April 1881, p. 1; "City and Country," *Manitoba Free Press* (Winnipeg), 27 Feb. 1890, p. 8; "City and Country," *Manitoba Free Press* (Winnipeg), 9 April 1890, p. 8.

114 Charles E. Goad, *Atlas of Brandon, Manitoba* (Montreal, Toronto: Charles E. Goad, rev. ed. 1913), Pl. 9; the authors are grateful to Donna Dul, Historic Resources Branch, Department of Tourism, Recreation and Cultural Affairs, Province of Manitoba, and Ed Young, Provincial Municipal Assessment Branch, Department of Municipal Affairs, Province of Manitoba for their help in researching this building.

115 *Henderson's North-Western Ontario, Manitoba and Northwest Directory and Gazetteer* (Winnipeg: James Henderson, 1888), pp. 403–4; the authors are grateful to Ella F. Chase, Emerson, Manitoba, and Marvis Sigurdson, Secretary-Treasurer, Town of Emerson, for their kind assistance in researching this terrace.

116 Charles E. Goad, *Insurance Plan of Edmonton, Alberta* (Toronto: Charles E. Goad, rev. ed. 1914), Vol. 1, sheet 10; *Henderson's Edmonton Directory* (Edmonton: Henderson Directories Alberta, 1910–75).

117 Personal communication from Mr. and Mrs. Gordon Glenn, Indian Head, Saskatchewan, Dec. 1977.

118 Terry Reksten, unpublished research notes on 1124 Fort Street, Victoria, Aug. 1977.

119 Terry Reksten, unpublished research notes on 507 Head Street, Esquimalt, Aug. 1977.

Bibliography

Arthur, Eric
Toronto No Mean City. University of Toronto Press, Toronto, 1974.

Association of Ontario Land Surveyors
Annual Report of the Association of Ontario Land Surveyors. Toronto, 1915. No. 30.

Atwood, Daniel Topping
Atwood's Modern American Homesteads. A.J. Bicknell & Company, New York, 1876.

Benoit, Dom
Vie de Mgr Taché. Librairie Beauchemin, Montreal, 1904. Vol. 2.

Bicknell, Amos Jackson
Bicknell's Public Buildings. A.J. Bicknell & Company, New York, 1878.

Bidou, Henry
Paris. Trans. J. Lewis May. Johnathan Cape, London, 1939.

Blakeley, Phyliss R.
Glimpses of Halifax. Public Archives of Nova Scotia, Halifax, 1949.

Bond, Courtney C.J.
City on the Ottawa. Queen's Printer, Ottawa, 1961.

Boston. Committee on Public Buildings.
The City Hall, Boston. City Council, Boston, 1866.

Brault, Lucien
Ottawa Old and New. Ottawa Historical Information Institute Ottawa, 1949.

Brosseau, Mathilde and David McConnell
"The Stations of the Intercolonial Railway, 1867–1914: Screening Paper." Manuscript on file, National Historic Parks and Sites Branch, Parks Canada, Ottawa, 1974.

Cameron, Christina
"47 Dalhousie Street, Quebec: CIHB Report"; "950–964 Saint-Jean Street, Quebec: CIHB Report." Manuscripts on file, National Historic Parks and Sites Branch, Parks Canada, Ottawa, 1972.

Canada. Department of Public Works.
Annual Report of the Minister of Public Works. Queen's Printer, Ottawa, 1871–83. Title varies.
General Report of the Minister of Public Works from 30 June, 1867, to 30 June, 1882. Queen's Printer, Ottawa, 1883.
General Report of the Minister of Public Works for the Fiscal Year ending 30 June 1878. Queen's Printer, Ottawa, 1878.

Canada. Public Archives.
RG11, Public Works Records, Vols. 291–92, subject 800–1, Correspondence relating to Post Office, Ottawa, 1860–74; Vols. 307–9, subject 881, Correspondence relating to Public Buildings, Toronto, 1860–74; Vols. 314–15, subject 884, Correspondence relating to Post Office, Toronto, 1860–74; Vols. 363–67, subject 993, Correspondence relating to Public Buildings, B.C., 1871–74; Vol. 841, exhibits 62–63, Semper Paratus to F.P. Rubidge, proposal for Parliament Buildings, n.d.; Vol. 3919, Specifications for Public Buildings A–M, 1871–87
RG12, Department of Transport Records, Intercolonial Railway, Vol. 1913, No. 3316–5, Correspondence relating to ICR Terminal, Halifax

Canada. Public Archives. National Map Collection.
H3/240–St. John–[1882], Bird's eye view of St. John, New Brunswick, O.H. Bailey, 1882
H2/340–Sherbrooke–1881, Bird's eye view of Sherbrooke, P.Q., 1881
H3/440–Brantford–[1875], Bird's eye view of Brantford, Ontario. Drawn by H. Brosius, Chas. Schoder, Prop's Chicago Lith., 1875

***Canadian Illustrated News* (Montreal)**
1869–83
"Barron Block," 27 Aug. 1870, p. 130;
"Vice-Regal Visit to Montreal," 23 Feb. 1878, pp. 119, 121.

Canadian Illustrated News Portfolio and Dominion Guide
Geo. E. Desbarats, Montreal, 1873.

City Directory of Toronto
Might Directories, Toronto, 1889–1976. Title varies.

"City Market Building, Saint John: Screening Paper"
Manuscript on file, National Historic Parks and Sites Branch, Parks Canada, Ottawa, 1970.

City of Victoria Heritage Advisory Committee
City of Victoria. City of Victoria, Victoria, 1974.

Coats, Douglas
"Calgary: The Private Schools, 1900–16." In *Frontier Calgary*, ed. A.W. Rasporick and H.C. Klassen, University of Calgary, McClelland and Stewart West, Calgary, 1975.

Cochrane, William, ed.
The Canadian Album: Men of Canada. Bradley, Carretson, Brantford, Ontario, 1891.

Conwell, Russell H.
History of the Great Fire of St. John, June 20 and 21, 1877. B.B. Russel, Boston, 1877.

Couillard-Després, Abbé A.
Histoire de Sorel. Imprimerie des sourds-muets, Montreal, 1926.

Croff, Gilbert Bostwick
Model Suburban Architecture, Embodying Designs for Dwellings of Moderate Cost. Roby & O'Neil, New York [1870].

Progressive American Architecture. Orange Judd & Company, New York [1875].

Cummings, Marcus Fayette
Cummings' Architectural Details. Orange Judd & Company, New York, 1873.

Cummings, Marcus Fayette and Charles Crosby Miller
Modern American Architecture. The authors, A.J. Bicknell, general agent, Troy, New York, 1868.

***Daily Acadian Recorder* (Halifax)**
"The New Intercolonial Railway Depot," 28 July 1877, p. [1].

***Daily Telegraph* (Saint John, N.B.)**
"A Handsome French Cottage," 14 Nov. 1877, p. [3];
"The Saint John Custom House," 26 April 1881, pp. [1–2];
"The Old and the New: Provincial Court House and Jail," 2 Oct. 1878, p. 3.

***Daily Witness* (Montreal)**
"Opening of New Windsor Hotel," 28 Jan. 1878, p. 8;
"The Windsor Hotel," "The Vice-Regal Visit," 15 Feb. 1878, p. 4.

Davies, William
Letters of William Davies, 1854–61. Ed. William Sherwood Fox. University of Toronto Press, Toronto, 1945.

De Bellaigue, Geoffrey
"Queen Victoria Buys French in 1855." *The Antique Collector* Vol. 46, No. 4 (April 1975), pp. 37–41. London.

De Volpi, Charles P. and P.S. Winkworth
Montreal: Recueil iconographique/A Pictorial Record. Dev-Sco Publications, Montreal, 1963. Vol. 2.

D'Iberville-Moreau, Luc
Lost Montreal. Oxford University Press, Toronto, 1975.

***Dominion Guide* (Montreal)**
7 June 1873, p. 354.

***Dominion Illustrated* (Montreal)**
1888–91.
"Special Number Devoted to Ottawa and the Parliament of Canada." Sabiston Litho. and Publishing, Montreal, 1891;
"The Metropolis of the Eastern Townships," 30 Aug. 1890;
"A Word from Wellington Street," 21 July 1888, p. 35.

Dufferin and Ava, Hariot Georgina (Hamilton) Hamilton-Temple-Blackwood, marchioness of
My Canadian Journal 1872–1878. Ed. Gladys Chantler Walker. Longmans Canada, Don Mills, Ontario, 1969.

Earle, Allison
"Quinniapiac, 25 Winter Avenue, Saint John's: CIHB Report." "49 Rennies Mill Road, Saint John's: CIHB Report." Manuscripts on file, National Historic Parks and Sites Branch, Parks Canada, Ottawa, 1974.

Eastern Townships Banks
Charter and Annual Reports, 1859–1912. Sherbrooke, 1912.

L'Encylopédie des styles d'hier et d'aujourd'hui
Marabout service, Paris, 1969. 2 vols. Vol. 2.

***Evening Telegram* (Saint John's, Nfld.)**
"A $20,000 Residence: Mr. Marshall's Magnificent Cottage," 23 March 1885, p. 2.

***Examiner* (Charlottetown)**
2 June 1877.

Flemming, David
A History of the Town of Niagara-on-the-Lake (1791–1970). Manuscript Report Series No. 25, Parks Canada, Ottawa, 1971.

Fletcher, Banister
A History of Architecture on the Comparative Method. 14th ed. C. Scribner & Sons, New York, 1948.
A History of Architecture on the Comparative Method. 17th ed. Athlone Press, University of London, London, 1961.

Freeman, John Crosby
"The Other Victoria." *Revue d'art canadienne/Canadian Art Review*, Vol. 1, No. 1 (1974), pp. 37–46. Quebec.

Gardner, Eugene Clarence
The House that Jill Built, After Jack's Had Proved a Failure. Fords, Howard & Hulbert, New York, 1882.

Gayle, Margot and Edmund Gillon
Cast-iron Architecture in New York. Dover Publications, New York, 1974.

***Gazette* (Montreal)**
Article on the Windsor Hotel, 29 Jan. 1878, p. 2.

***Gazette* (Sherbrooke)**
"Local and Other Items," 9 April 1875, p. [3].

Giroux, André
"3532–3538 Sainte-Famille Street, Montreal: CIHB Report." Manuscript on file, National Historic Parks and Sites Branch, Parks Canada, Ottawa, 1972.

Goad, Charles E.
Atlas of Brandon, Manitoba. Charles E. Goad, Toronto, rev. ed. 1913.
Atlas of City of Montreal. Charles E. Goad, Toronto, Montreal, 1881.
Atlas of the City of Toronto. Charles E. Goad, Montreal, 1884.
Insurance Atlas of the City of Ottawa. Charles E. Goad, Toronto, rev. ed. 1895.

Insurance Plan of Edmonton, Alberta. Charles E. Goad, Toronto, rev. ed. 1914. Vol. 1.

Godey's Lady's Book
Vols. 86, 93–96 (1873, 1876–78). Philadelphia.

Guillet, Edwin C.
Pioneer Inns and Taverns. Ontario Publishing, Toronto, 1956 Vol. 2.

Gowans, Alan
Building Canada: An Architectural History of Canadian Life. Oxford University Press, Toronto, 1966.
Images of American Living; Four Centuries of Architecture and Furniture as Cultural Expression. J.B. Lippincott, Philadelphia, 1964.

Greenhill, R., K. Macpherson and D. Richardson
Ontario Towns. Oberon Press, Ottawa, 1974.

Hale, C. Anne
"City Market Building, Saint John: CIHB Report"; "The Legislative Building, Fredericton: CIHB Report"; "767 Brunswick Street, Fredericton: CIHB Report"; "354 Main Street, Saint John: CIHB Report"; "99 Wentworth Street, Saint John: CIHB Report"; "Report on D.E. Dunham." Manuscripts on file, National Historic Parks and Sites Branch, Parks Canada, Ottawa, 1974.

Hammett, Ralph W.
Architecture in the United States: A Survey of Architectural Styles Since 1776. John Wiley & Sons, New York, 1976.

Henderson's Directory of the City of Winnipeg
James Henderson, Winnipeg, 1880–1912.

Henderson's Edmonton Directory
Henderson Directories Alberta, Edmonton, 1910–75.

Henderson's North-Western Ontario, Manitoba and Northwest Directory and Gazetteer
James Henderson, Winnipeg, 1888.

Hersey, George L.
"Godey's Choice." *Journal of the Society of Architectural Historians*, Vol. 18, No. 3 (Oct. 1959), pp. 104–11. Philadelphia.

Historical Atlas Publishing Company
Historical Atlas of Wellington County. Reprint of 1906 ed. Corporation of the County of Wellington, Wellington County, 1972.

Hitchcock, Henry-Russell
Architecture: Nineteenth and Twentieth Centuries. Penguin Books, Harmondsworth, Middlesex, 1958.
"Second Empire 'avant la lettre'." *Gazette des beaux-arts*, Vol. 42 ([Aug.] 1953), pp. 115–30. Paris.

Hobbs, Isaac H. and Son
Hobbs's Architecture: Containing Designs and Ground Plans for Villas, Cottages and other Edifices, both Suburban and Rural. J.B. Lippincott & Company, Philadelphia, 1873.

Holly, Henry Hudson
Holly's Country Seats. D. Appleton & Company, New York, 1863.

Horrors in Architecture and So-called Works of Art in Bronze in the City of New York ... By an Admirer of Art Whose Name is no Consequence to the Reader
N.p., New York, 1886.

Howard, W.H.
Halifax of Today: An Illustrated Souvenir of the Queen's Diamond Jubilee 1837–97. W.H. Howard, Halifax, 1897.

Hurd, Henry M., ed.
The Institutional Care of the Insane in the United States and Canada. Arno Press, New York, 1973. Vol. 4.

Hussey, Elisha Charles
Hussey's National Cottage Architecture. Geo. E. Woodward, New York, 1874.
Home Building. A Reliable Book of Facts, Relating to Building, Living, Materials, Costs. Leader & Van Hoesen, New York [1876].

Ingram, J.S.
The Centennial Exposition Described and Illustrated. Hubbard Bros., Philadelphia [1876].

Jack, David Russell
"Book Plates," *Acadiensis*, Vol. 1, No. 2 (April 1901), pp. 96–97. St. John N.B.

Kalman, Harold
Exploring Vancouver. University of British Columbia Press, Vancouver, 1974.

Kennion, John W.
The Architects' and Builders' Guide. Fitzpatrick & Hunter, New York, 1868.

Kerr, Donald
"Vancouver – A Study in Human Geography." MA thesis, University of Toronto, Toronto, 1943.

Lakey, Charles D.
Lakey's Village and Country Houses. American Builder Publishing Company, New York, 1875.

Lambert, Phyllis and Robert Lemire
Inventaire des bâtiments du vieux Montréal, du quartier Saint-Antoine et de la ville de Maisonneuve construits entre 1880 et 1915. Ministère des Affaires culturelles, Quebec, 1977. Dossier 25.

Langsam, Walter E.
"Thomas Fuller and Augustus Laver: Victorian Neo-Baroque and Second Empire vs. Gothic Revival in North America." *Journal of the Society of Architectural Historians*, Vol. 29, No. 3 (Oct. 1970), p. 270.

Leblond de Brumath, A.
Guide de Montréal et de ses environs. Granger Frères, Montreal, 1897.

Lemoine, James M.
Picturesque Quebec. Dawson Brothers, Montreal, 1882.

Loring, Sanford E.
Principles and Practices of Architecture. Cobb, Pritchard & Company, Chicago, 1869.

Lovell's Montreal Directory
John Lovell, Montreal, 1872–78.

Lutman, John
"534 Queens Avenue, London: CIHB Report." Manuscript on file, National Historic Parks and Sites Branch, Parks Canada, Ottawa, 1974.

Madoc Review
Way Back When. Pigden and McKinnon, Madoc, Ont., 1976.

Manitoba Free Press (Winnipeg)
"The Building Boom," 12 April 1881, p. 1;
"City and Country," 27 Feb. 1890, p. 8;
"City and Country," 9 April 1890, p. 8.

Marsan, Jean-Claude
Montréal en évolution. Fides, Montreal, 1974.

McAlpine's Halifax City Directory
McAlpine's Directories, Halifax, 1887–88, 1895–96.

McKenna, Rosalie Thorne
"James Renwick, Jr. and the Second Empire in the United States." *Magazine of Art*, Vol. 44, No. 3 (March 1951), pp. 97–101. New York.

Meacham, J.H. & Co.
Illustrated Historical Atlas of Prince Edward Island. Reprint of 1880 ed. Mika Silk Screening Ltd., Belleville, Ont., 1972.

Mercury (Guelph)
"110-Year-Old Guelph Home," 20 March 1976, n.p.;
"Goldie Home Sold: Fine Old Residence Changes Hands," June 1952, n.p.

Metropolitan Toronto Library Board. Canadiana and Manuscripts Section.
File on Government House, Toronto.

Mika, Mr. and Mrs. N.H.
"Phillips-Faulkner House, Belleville: Screening Paper." Manuscript on file, National Historic Parks and Sites Branch, Parks Canada, Ottawa, 1969.

Mills, G. Edward
"Masonic Temple, Victoria: CIHB Report"; "Custom House, 1002 Wharf Street, Victoria: CIHB Report." Manuscripts on file, National Historic Parks and Sites Branch, Parks Canada, Ottawa, 1975, 1976.

Mills, G. Edward and Janet Wright
"Victoria City Hall: Screening Paper." Manuscript on file, National Historic Parks and Sites Branch, Parks Canada, Ottawa, 1977.

Mirror (Digby, N.S.)
Article on the Queen Hotel, Annapolis Royal, 13 July 1977, p. 2.

Mitchell, R. and T.K. Thorlakson
"James Kerr, 1848–1911, and Henry Hyland Kerr, 1881–1963; Pioneer Canadian – American Surgeons." *Canadian Journal of Surgery*, Vol. 9 (July 1966), pp. 213–20.

Montreal. Archives nationales du Québec.
Greffe, C. Cushing, 3 Feb. 1874

Morisset, Gérard
"Le Parlement de Québec." *Habitat*, Vol. 3, No. 6 (Nov.–Dec. 1966), pp. 25–28. Ottawa.

Mulvany, C. Pelham
Toronto: Past and Present. W.E. Caiger, Toronto, 1884.

New Brunswick Reporter (Fredericton)
"The New Buildings," 31 March 1880, p. [2].

New Era (Clinton, Ont.)
24 Jan. 1878, n.p.

Newfoundland Historic Trust
A Gift of Heritage: Historic Architecture of St. John's. Newfoundland Historic Trust Publications, St. John's, 1975. Vol. 1.

Niagara-on-the-Lake, Canada
Town Council of Niagara-on-the-Lake, Niagara-on-the-Lake, Ont., n.d., p. 27.

Noppen, Luc
"L'architecture des parlements de Québec." *L'Action* (Quebec), 21 April 1973, pp. 1–3.

Nova Scotia. House of Assembly.
Journals of the House of Assembly. Queen's Printer, Halifax, 1878–79.

O'Dea, Shane
The Domestic Architecture of Old St. John's. Newfoundland Historical Society, St. John's, 1974. Pamphlet No. 2.

Ontario Gazetteer and Business Directory
R.L. Polk, Toronto, 1888–89.

L'Opinion publique (Montreal)
1870–83.
"L'asile d'aliénés de Falconwood," 23 March 1873, p. 146;
"Le Bloc Barron," 4 July 1872, pp. 316, 320.

Ottawa Directory and Dominion Guide
A.S. Woodburn, Ottawa, 1875.

Ottawa. Municipal Archives.
Minutes of Council for part of the years 1874, 1875, 1876 and 1877, pp.
185–86, 200.

Page and Smith
Illustrated Historical Atlas of the County of Wentworth, Ontario. Reprint of
1875 ed. Dundas Valley School of Art, Dundas, Ontario, 1971.

Palliser, Palliser & Company
Palliser's New Cottage, Homes and Details. Palliser, Palliser & Company,
New York [1887].

Pinkney, David H.
Napoleon III and the Rebuilding of Paris. Princeton University Press,
Princeton, N.J., 1958.

Preston, Richard Arthur
Canada's RMC: A History of the Royal Military College. University of
Toronto Press, Toronto, 1969.

Prince Edward Island. House of Assembly.
Journal of the House of Assembly. Queen's Printer, Charlottetown, 1878.

Progressive American Architecture
Orange Judd & Company, New York [1875].

Québec (City). Archives civiles.
Contract between John Hatch and the Y.M.C.A., Quebec, 21 Jan. 1879,
No. 9653
Greffe P. Huot, 9 June 1882. No. 8694; 10 June 1882, Nos. 8697, 8698,
8699

Québec. Archives du séminaire de Québec.
Journal du Séminaire, Vol. 2, 31 May 1875, 21 Oct. 1876

Quebec City Directory
Quebec, 1882–1930. Title and publisher vary.

Quebec Gazette
"Mansard Roofs," 20 Nov. 1872, p. [2].

Richardson, A.J.H.
"Guide to the Architecturally and Historically most Significant Buildings in
the Old City of Quebec." *Bulletin of the Association for Preservation
Technology*, Vol. 2, Nos. 3–4 (1970), pp. 3–144. Ottawa.

Richardson, Douglas
"The Spirit of the Place." *Canadian Antiques Collector*, Vol. 10, No. 5
(Sept.–Oct. 1975), pp. 20–29. Toronto.

Rogers, Irene
"Birchwood, 35 Longworth Avenue, Charlottetown: CIHB Report"; "Law
Courts Building, Charlottetown: CIHB Report." Manuscripts on file, Na-
tional Historic Parks and Sites Branch, Parks Canada, Ottawa, 1974.

Ross, Victor
The History of the Canadian Bank of Commerce. Oxford University Press,
Toronto, 1920. Vol. 1.

Rostecki, Randy R.
"The Rise and Demise of Winnipeg's Central Business District"; "Law
Courts Building, 391 Broadway, Winnipeg: CIHB Report." Manuscripts
on file, National Historic Parks and Sites, Parks Canada, Ottawa, 1976.

Royal Gazette and Newfoundland Advertiser (St. John's)
"Laying Foundation Stone of Athenaeum," 9 Nov. 1875, p. [2].

Saint John Daily News (N.B.)
"Reopening of Saint John's Church," 25 Nov. 1872, p. [3].

Saunders, Ivan
"395–409 Alexander Avenue, Winnipeg: CIHB Report." Manuscript on
file, National Historic Parks and Sites Branch, Parks Canada, Ottawa,
1974.

Schull, Joseph
100 Years of Banking: A History of the Toronto Dominion Bank. Copp
Clark, Toronto, 1958.

**"Shaughnessy House, 1923 Dorchester Street West, Montreal:
Screening Paper."**
Manuscript on file, National Historic Parks and Sites Branch, Parks Can-
ada, Ottawa, 1973.

Sloan, Samuel
*Sloan's Homestead Architecture, Containing Forty Designs for Villas,
Cottages, and Farmhouses, with Essays on Style, Construction, Landscape Gardening, Furniture, etc., etc.* J.B. Lippincott & Company, Philadelphia, 1861.

Smallwood, Joseph R., ed.
The Book of Newfoundland. Newfoundland Book Publishers, St. John's,
1967. Vol. 4.

Smithmeyer, John L.
Our Architecture and its Defects. C.W. Brown, Washington, D.C., 1880.

Sommer, Warren
"Yale Hotel, Vancouver: CIHB Report." Manuscript on file, National
Historic Parks and Sites Branch, Parks Canada, Ottawa, 1975.

Steen, W.D. and E.E. Boyce
Winnipeg, Manitoba and her Industries. Steen and Boyce, Winnipeg, 1882.

Stewart, J. Douglas
"Architecture for a Boom Town: The Primitive and the Neo-Baroque in George Browne's Kingston Buildings," in *To Preserve and Defend: Essays on Kingston in the Nineteenth Century*, ed. Gerald Tulchinsky, McGill-Queen's University Press, Montreal, 1976.

Toronto City Directory
R.L. Polk Directories, Toronto, 1887–88.

Toronto. Toronto Historical Board.
File on 3 Meredith Crescent, Toronto.

Truro, Nova Scotia: The Hub of the Province
James Bayne, Grand Rapids, Mich., n.d.

Vancouver Daily World
Illustrated Souvenir Publication. Vancouver Daily World, Vancouver, 1891.

Vaux, Calvert
Villas and Cottages. Harper & Brothers, New York, 1857.

Whiffen, Marcus
American Architecture Since 1780: A Guide to the Styles. MIT Press, Cambridge, Mass., 1969.

Winnipeg Daily Sun
"The Old and The New: Provincial Court House and Jail," 20 Jan. 1883, p. 8;
"The Building Boom," 20 Oct. 1883, p. 3;
"The Bull's Eye: Great Growth of Winnipeg," 30 Oct. 1883, p. 3.

Withey, Henry P. and Elsie R. Withey
Biographical Dictionary of American Architects (Deceased). New Age Publishing Company, Los Angeles, 1956.

Wodehouse, Lawrence
"Alfred B. Mullett and his French Style Government Buildings." *Journal of the Society of Architectural Historians*, Vol. 31, No. 1 (March 1972), pp. 22–37. Philadelphia.

Woodley, E.C.
The House of Joseph in the Life of Quebec. N.p., Quebec, 1946.

Woodward, George Evertson
Woodward's National Architect; Containing 1,000 Original Designs, Plans and Details, to Working Scale, for the Practical Construction of Dwelling Houses for the Country, Suburb and Village. Geo. E. Woodward, New York [1869].

Canadian Historic Sites:
Occasional Papers in Archaeology and History

1 *Archaeological Investigations of the National Historic Sites Service, 1962–1966*, John H. Rick; *A Classification System for Glass Beads for the Use of Field Archaeologists*, K.E. and M.A. Kidd; *The Roma Settlement at Brudenell Point, Prince Edward Island*, Margaret Coleman. $4.00; $4.80 outside Canada.

2 *Contributions from the Fortress of Louisbourg* – No. 1 *Archaeological Research at the Fortress of Louisbourg, 1961–1965*, Edward McM. Larrabee; *A "Rescue Excavation" at the Princess Half-Bastion, Fortress of Louisbourg*, Bruce W. Fry; *An Archaeological Study of Clay Pipes from the King's Bastion, Fortress of Louisbourg*, Iain C. Walker. $4.00; $4.80 outside Canada.

3 *Comparisons of the Faunal Remains from French and British Refuse Pits at Fort Michilimackinac: A Study in Changing Subsistence Patterns*, Charles E. Cleland; *The French in Gaspé, 1534 to 1760*, David Lee; *The Armstrong Mound on Rainy River, Ontario*, Walter A. Kenyon. $3.00; $3.60 outside Canada.

4 *A Brief History of Lower Fort Garry*, Dale Miquelon; *The Big House, Lower Fort Garry*, George C. Ingram; *Industrial and Agricultural Activities at Lower Fort Garry*, George C. Ingram; *The Sixth Regiment of Foot at Fort Garry*, William R. Morrison; *The Second Battalion, Quebec Rifles, at Lower Fort Garry*, William R. Morrison. $4.00; $4.80 outside Canada.

5 *Excavations at Lower Fort Garry, 1965–1967; A General Description of Excavations and Preliminary Discussions*, James V. Chism. $3.00; $3.60 outside Canada.

6 *A History of Rocky Mountain House*, Hugh A. Dempsey; *The Excavation and Historical Identification of Rocky Mountain House*, William C. Noble. $3.00; $3.60 outside Canada.

7 *Archaeological Investigations at Signal Hill, Newfoundland, 1965–66*, Edward B. Jelks. $3.00; $3.60 outside Canada.

8 *The Canals of Canada*, John P. Heisler. $5.00; $6.00 outside Canada.

9 *The Canadian Lighthouse*, Edward F. Bush; *Table Glass Excavated at Fort Amherst, Prince Edward Island*, Paul McNally; *Halifax Waterfront Buildings: A Historical Report*, Susan Buggey. $7.75; $9.30 outside Canada.

10 *The Architectural Heritage of the Rideau Corridor*, Barbara A. Humphreys; *Glassware Excavated at Fort Gaspereau, New Brunswick*, Jane E. Harris; *Commissioners of the Yukon, 1897–1918*, Edward F. Bush. $5.00; $6.00 outside Canada.

11 *The Battle of Queenston Heights*, Carol Whitfield, *A History of Fort George, Upper Canada*, Robert S. Allen; *The Battle of Châteauguay*, Victor J.H. Suthren. $5.00; $6.00 outside Canada.

12 *Contributions from the Fortress of Louisbourg* – No. 2 *Lime Preparation at 18th-Century Louisbourg*, Charles S. Lindsay; *Louisbourg Guardhouses*, Charles S. Lindsay; *A Survey of Louisbourg Gunflints*, T.M. Hamilton and Bruce W. Fry. $5.00; $6.00 outside Canada.

13 *All That Glitters: A Memorial to Ottawa's Capitol Theatre and Its Predecessors*, Hilary Russell; *Glassware Excavated at Beaubassin, Nova Scotia*, Jane E. Harris; *Sir Sam Hughes (1853–1921)*, Carol Whitfield. $6.50; $7.80 outside Canada.

14 *The British Indian Department and the Frontier in North America, 1755–1830*, Robert S. Allen; *The B.C. Mills Prefabricated System: The Emergence of Ready-Made Buildings in Western Canada*, G.E. Mills and D.W. Holdsworth. $5.75; $6.90 outside Canada.

15 *A History of Martello Towers in the Defence of British North America, 1796–1871*, Ivan J. Saunders; *Report of the 1972 Archaeological Excavations of the Market Shoal Tower, Kingston, Ontario*, Donald A. Harris. $6.75; $8.10 outside Canada.

16 *The Battle of the Restigouche*, Judith Beattie and Bernard Pothier; *Table Glass from the Wreck of the* Machault, Paul McNally; *The Western European Coarse Earthenwares from the Wreck of the* Machault, K.J. Barton; *The Cochrane Ranch*, William Naftel. $5.00; $6.00 outside Canada.

17 *The Halifax Citadel, 1825–60: A Narrative and Structural History*, John Joseph Greenough. $6.00; $7.20 outside Canada.

18   *Contributions from the Fortress of Louisbourg* – No. 3
A Campaign of Amateurs: The Siege of Louisbourg, 1745, Raymond F. Baker; *The Construction and Occupation of the Barracks of the King's Bastion at Louisbourg*, Blaine Adams. $6.50; $7.80 outside Canada.

19   *Yukon Transportation: A History*, Gordon Bennett. $6.50; $7.80 outside Canada.

20   *The History of Fort Langley, 1827–96*, Mary K. Cullen; *Ranch Houses of the Alberta Foothills*, L.G. Thomas. $6.50; $7.80 outside Canada.

21   *The First Contingent: The North-West Mounted Police, 1873–74*, Philip Goldring; *Whisky, Horses and Death: The Cypress Hills Massacre and its Sequel*, Philip Goldring; *The Dawson Daily News: Journalism in the Klondike*, Edward F. Bush. $6.50; $7.80 outside Canada.

22   *Spode/Copeland Transfer-Printed Patterns Found at 20 Hudson's Bay Company Sites*, Lynne Sussman. $10.00; $12.00 outside Canada.

23   *Blockhouses in Canada, 1749–1841: A Comparative Report and Catalogue*, Richard J. Young; *Gaspé, 1760–1867*, David Lee. $10.00; $12.00 outside Canada.

24   *Second Empire Style in Canadian Architecture*, Christina Cameron and Janet Wright. $10.00; $12.00 outside Canada.

History and Archaeology/Histoire et archéologie

Publications available in Canada through authorized bookstore agents and other bookstores, or by mail from the Canadian Government Publishing Centre, Supply and Services Canada, Hull, Quebec, Canada K1A 0S9.

5   *A Report on a West Coast Whaling Canoe Reconstructed at Port Renfrew, B.C.*, E.Y. Arima. 1975. $5.50; $6.50 outside Canada.

6   *Louisbourg and the Indians: A Study in Imperial Race Relations, 1713–1760*, Olive Patricia Dickason; *Surgeons and Surgery in Ile Royale*, Linda M. Hoad. 1976. $10.50; $12.60 outside Canada.

7   *Archaeology and the Fur Trade: The Excavation of Sturgeon Fort, Saskatchewan*, Norman F. and Anne Barka. 1976. $6.25; $7.50 outside Canada.

8   *Navy Hall, Niagara-on-the-Lake*, David Flemming; *Fort Wellington: A Structural History*, David Lee; *The Battle of the Windmill: November 1838*, David Lee. 1976. $5.75; $6.90 outside Canada.

9   *Fort George on the Niagara: An Archaeological Perspective*, John P. Wilson and Linda D. Southwood. 1976. $8.00; $9.60 outside Canada.

11   *Clay Tobacco-Pipes, with Particular Reference to the Bristol Industry*, Iain C. Walker. 1977. 4 vols. $25.00; $30.00 outside Canada.

12   *Prehistoric Occupations at Coteau-du-Lac, Quebec: A Mixed Assemblage of Archaic and Woodland Artifacts*, Richard Lueger; *Analyses of Two Prehistoric Copper Artifacts from the Cloverleaf Bastion of the Fort at Coteau-du-Lac, Quebec*, A. Couture and J.O. Edwards; *Identification of Representative Prehistoric Stone Artifacts and Samples of Unworked Stone from the Cloverleaf Bastion of the Fort at Coteau-du-Lac, Quebec*, D.E. Lawrence; *Fish Remains from the Cloverleaf Bastion of the Fort at Coteau-du-Lac, Quebec*, W.B. Scott; *The Human Osteological Material from the Cloverleaf Bastion of the Fort at Coteau-du-Lac, Quebec*, J. Edson Way. 1977. $8.00; $9.60 outside Canada.

13   *The American Capture of Fort George, Ontario*, Margaret Coleman; *The Guardhouse at Fort George, Ontario*, Elizabeth Vincent. 1977. $7.25; $8.70 outside Canada.

14   *A Study of Fort St. Joseph*, J.N. Emerson, H.E. Devereux, M.J. Ashworth. 1977. $9.50; $11.40 outside Canada.

15   *Glimpses of Soldiering at Coteau-du-Lac, Quebec – 1780 to 1856*, Karen Price; *Beads from the Fort at Coteau-du-Lac, Quebec*, Karlis Karklins; *Table Glass from the Fort at Coteau-du-Lac, Quebec*, Paul McNally; *Coins from the Fort at Coteau-du-Lac, Quebec*, Ann Cunningham Falvey. 1977. $8.25; $9.90 outside Canada.

16   *Cumulative Seriation and Ceramic Formula Dating: A Preliminary Study*, Roger T. Grange, Jr. 1977. $4.25; $5.10 outside Canada.

18   *Early Fortification Ditches at Ile-aux-Noix, Quebec*, Roger T. Grange, Jr. 1977. 2 vols. $5.50; $6.60 outside Canada.

19   *Excavation of the Porter's Cottage, Civilian Barracks/Straw Shed, Northern Mounds and Rampart at Fort Lennox National Historic Park, 1966*, Roger T. Grange, Jr. 1978. $5.50; $6.60 outside Canada.

20   *The Archaeology of Fort Lennox, Ile-aux-Noix, Quebec, 1964 Season*, Norman F. Barka; *The Beads from Fort Lennox, Quebec*, Karlis Karklins. 1978. $7.75; $9.30 outside Canada.

21   *An Annotated Bibliography for the Study of Building Hardware*, Peter J. Priess. 1978. $2.75; $3.30 outside Canada.

22   *Fishing Methods Used in the St. Lawrence River and Gulf*, Marcel Moussette. 1979. $6.75; $8.10 outside Canada.

23   *The British Garrison in Quebec City as Described in Newspapers from 1764 to 1840*, Claudette Lacelle. 1979. $4.50; $5.40 outside Canada.

24   *The Ceramics of Lower Fort Garry: Operations 1 to 31*, Lynne Sussman. 1979. $8.00; $9.60 outside Canada.

25 *A Study of Surface-Mounted Door Locks from a Number of Archaeological Sites in Canada*, Peter J. Priess; *Inverarden: Retirement Home of Fur Trader John McDonald of Garth*, Robert J. Burns. 1979. $8.00; $9.60 outside Canada.

26 *The Military History of Placentia: A Study of the French Fortifications*, Jean-Pierre Proulx; *Placentia: 1713–1811*, Jean-Pierre Proulx. 1979. $8.00; $9.60 outside Canada.

27 *Nineteenth-Century Glassware from the Roma Site, Prince Edward Island*, Jeanne Alyluia; *Cutlery from the Roma Site, Prince Edward Island*, Barbara J. Wade. 1979. $7.25; $8.70 outside Canada.

28 *The Soldiers of Isle Royale*, Allan Greer. 1979. $5.00; $6.00 outside Canada.

29 *French Table Glass from the Fortress of Louisbourg, Nova Scotia*, Paul McNally; *Eighteenth-Century French Blue-Green Bottles from the Fortress of Louisbourg, Nova Scotia*, Jane E. Harris. 1979. $7.50; $9.00 outside Canada.

30 *Glass Bead-Making from the Middle Ages to the Early 19th Century*, Kenneth E. Kidd. 1979. $5.00; $6.00 outside Canada.